She Never Said Good-bye

She Never Said Good-bye

One man's journey through loss

ROBERT DYKSTRA

Harold Shaw Publishers
Wheaton, Illinois

Library of Congress Cataloging-in-Publication Data
Dykstra, Robert, 1932-
  She never said good-bye.
    1. Bereavement—Religious aspects—Christianity.
2. Consolation. 3. Dykstra, Robert, 1932-   .
I. Title.
BV4905.2.D95 1989   248.8'6   88-31996
ISBN 0-87788-759-4

98 97 96 95 94 93 92 91 90 89
10 9 8 7 6 5 4 3 2 1

Contents

Contents

Foreword

Perhaps you should be warned as you begin reading this book that it will "grab" you. It did me. In fact you will scarcely be able to leave off reading until the last page.

It is almost harsh in its honesty and forthrightness. Indeed, we have here the acute lamentation of a human soul in torment, not entirely because of grief, but frustration that in infancy his wife had suffered mistreatment that resulted finally in capitulation to mental suffering.

You may, as I did, read portions of the book through tears. At times the author storms at just about everything and everyone, including himself, as we all do at one time or another. But few of us travel through such extreme, life-shattering experiences. Nor does he spare the church in which he has for years been an effective minister. Devotion to the church is here laced with resentment, ambivalently resulting from the tragedy of his wife's suicide.

The author seems to be fighting his way to normal life through extreme mental suffering. One follows this soul's profoundly moving agony with sympathy and understanding, though perhaps not with full comprehension. This latter cannot perhaps be achieved vicariously.

Seldom do we encounter such complete self-revelation as in this book. We find ourselves feeling deeply for a man who puts on paper just about everything he thinks and feels as he passes through a dark and terrible valley. We feel admiration, too, for obviously he possesses inner strength fueled by faith which keeps rationality solvent through all poignant questioning and frustration.

Mr. Dykstra tells us that he wrote the book only for himself. But if any troubled and unhappy person walking the stormy way with him should find peace at last, he will be pleased indeed.

Norman Vincent Peale

Acknowledgments

I wish to thank colleagues in the ministry who encouraged me to publish this work—Vernon Dethmers, John Egy, and Professor Paul Fries of New Brunswick Theological Seminary. I also owe a word of thanks to John Van Spronson who kept me supplied with reading material during the last year and with whom I could and did discuss on both a personal and philosophical level what I've been trying to say; and to Ingrid Steele, who typed and re-typed the manuscript, after making invaluable suggestions. And I thank the members of the congregation of the Reformed Church in Saddle Brook, New Jersey, who loved my wife, bore with me their own grief, and listened to my preaching, some of which found its way into this book. Finally, I thank my daughters, Deborah and Elizabeth, whose affection for their mother confirms my conviction that she was a very special person whom we shall always miss.

Preface

In 1984, a week following Thanksgiving Day, Yvonne, my wife of thirty years, took her own life. She gave me no perceptible warnings; she left no notes. The anguish that followed was a journey for which I never could have been prepared and one which I made essentially alone. There was so little anyone could do for me. Few are skilled enough to deal with grief, and fewer still dare penetrate its darkest corners. Even we pastors, ministers of the Word, are miserable comforters.

During that bleak isolation I was able to stay in touch with my own feelings by jotting down in my journal all the persistent questions, the plaguing thoughts, the mixed emotions, the seemingly futile prayers for which there could be no clear answers. From that record this book evolved. I wrote it to fulfill my own crying need to assuage some of the pain, and, for want of a more fitting description of my task, to avenge her death. If this helps others though their dark night of sorrow and despair, so much the better.

Robert Dykstra
Saddle Brook, New Jersey

1

The Lonely Journey

Grief is a solitary task. You work at it alone, or with those few companions of your deliberate choice. I am walking through the park with my Labrador, Luke, and with my thoughts. Luke, the beloved physician, the gentle evangelist, the hospital saint, my constant companion.

He breaks windows with his heavy snout and sheds bales of black wool throughout the house, yet Luke is still a healing presence. He is no evangelist telling good news, no bearer of tender stories, no careful historian like his bibiical namesake. He carries mud on his feet and quarts of saliva pour from his tongue and jowls, but he brings me, in this solitude, the weighty, wordless companionship I need.

This is a rare walk I take with Luke this morning; I have done little of it since she's been gone. I'd rather stay in bed, trying to make up for another of those fitful, sleepless nights; waiting for the winter sun to rise high enough to brighten my room and shine me out of my stupor. But the shades are drawn and the sun has no way to pierce the heavy cloud cover anyway. Even if it were to dazzle my room, I doubt it would arouse me. A leaden dullness drags upon my spirit. The gray ghosts hound me, track me down, dog my every step.

Luke and I press on through the lightly falling snow. No wind blows at this early hour and the temperature has climbed just enough for snow to fall. The thermometer threatens, however, to plunge tonight, so this morning offers a singular opportunity to take a winter walk. Both our noses are cold and wet; the blood begins to tingle in fingertips and toes. A lone cross-country skier schusses by. He and I exchange pleasantries; Luke pays no heed. The skier and I are in a world of sight and dim images, words and symbols. Luke lives in a world of scent, picking up the old signs and odors of dogs and bitches, checking out every tree and bush, marking each with his unique signature.

He runs free, romping through the snow, testing the world with his nose. The falling flakes turn his obsidian coat to a pale gray, blending it with all the shades of gray that pencil

2

in our snowy and dreary day. He shakes his entire body; a blizzard of crystals fills the air, swirling in a white shroud around him. Some stick to the thick mat of oily fur, melting and refreezng to ice, and hang from his hocks, shading his brown eyes. Drifts cling to his heavy nape and form a ski slope at the base of his tail. Showing no discomfort, he gambols across the park lawns.

I am growing warm now, thankful I didn't add a woolen sweater under my down parka. The small of my back is wet with perspiration. Now I am committed to keep walking, to press on, not to stop until I'm home where it's warm and dry. Joggers and runners pass by on the path, steaming and snorting like locomotives, pressing waffle prints in the new snow, flashing fancy pants and names: Etonic, Adidas, Reebok, Saucony. Some are in groups, talking as they run and pant. Most are alone, puffing for every breath, presumably thinking their own thoughts. I wonder what they can be thinking in their lonely flight.

Are they running on this cold January day simply because they enjoy running? Are they becoming so physically fit as to defy mortality? How they go, on and on! Or is this running a deeper sign of our times and are they trying to escape, doing precisely what I in my heart really feel like doing? I am happy I can at least walk these three miles on this winter day, considering my gimpy knees and clogged arteries. But my soul seeks to run from all that is and was and even from what is yet to come. Or, better yet, I'd love to fly, longing with the Psalmist "that I might take the wings of the morning."

Boisterous crows raise a ruckus in the grove of trees framing a residential street near the park. It sounds as if they are mobbing an owl resting there from his nightly hunting flight, sitting out this irritation in the heavy wood; or perhaps they are playing games with a red-tailed hawk, waiting silently, patiently for its prey. We don't stop to investigate; we press on, now with a wind rising, the snow blowing into face and muzzle. My glasses are beaded with melt-water and the landscape before me is blurred, liquefied into itself like an impressionistic painting, but without the color.

Gulls wheel and scream overhead, waiting for the Saturday bread-tossers to come to the park, when they can skillfully dive and steal a crust from some clumsy duck. A flock of park geese holler and cackle as they splash down into the river. A kestrel darts across the meadow, searching for its meal. There are no grasshoppers today. He will watch for a sparrow sitting atop a bramble bush or listen for the squeak of a vole clambering through a tussock of grass. He and I share the park together as fellow predators. Death feeds our lives and we survive on it; but neither of us thinks of it like that.

I do, however, think about death. Her death won't go away; it won't retreat from my mind. A million scenarios of her dying flash upon the screen of my imagination. There is not a bit of satisfaction in any of them; I attach credibility to none; not a one brings me any sense of hope or joy.

I feel from her death those feelings evoked from the lonely runner. Except for Luke, I am here alone with my painful thoughts. I muster every ounce of energy to keep going in circles around the park, only to come back to where I've always been. No one can run for me, nor even next to me. Only my Lab, who lives for this single dot on history's time-line, can trot at my heels. Otherwise my constant companions are death and absence—companions that neither hasten the journey nor carry for me the backpack crammed with my haunting thoughts and painful memories.

Only in my imagination do I stop. I pause to stand with those armies who wait at hospital bedsides, trying desperately to maneuver inconspicuously around the clutter of life-sustaining apparatus, listening to the slow click of metered machines, the rhythmic, hollow hiss of respirators. I understand their anguish that protests: "Why don't these doctors do something for him? Can't they find a new drug? Perform a life-saving surgery?" I remember my muted pleas: "Why can't you police, with all your radios and radar, your modern detection systems, your commitment to order, go out and find her?" "Why doesn't some hospital call me, tell me to come down, that she'll be all right?" "Why, on this darkest of nights, as my daughter and I wait out the hours in total helplessness, doesn't someone tenderly pick her up and bring her to safety—to me?"

No one does. We are all running down the park path alone, in circles, or to some far off, unknown place, to the edge of the earth.

If it is true that death condemns us to solitude, then it is equally true that suicide treats us like lepers, like pariahs. Not until after a month had passed did I realize that I was weeping to a tune different from all my companions. I was struggling with the sorrow of death and loss; they with the mystery of suicide. They were speechless, awkward, clumsy with both their words and looks. I felt pushed out of their lives and minds as though I were just one more irritating thorn in their flesh, one more annoying itch they couldn't seem to reach in order to scratch. That same itching pestilence came over me, occupying my thoughts and time, defying all my attempts to scratch.

Death in the late twentieth century has taken the place of sex in the nineteenth, according to A. Alvarez in his *A Savage God*. They are untouchable topics. In the old 1800s, death was as common as life: children, young adults as well as the aging, died, and that was accepted as a part of the human cycle. How new life and children came into the world was kept as a hidden secret. Today you can find sex out in the open like any supermarket commodity. You can pick it up in drug stores like cough drops, from a department store like a sweater, from the media like a weather report. But death hides somewhere under the counters and dares show its face only in the sleaziest neighborhoods.

In 1940, her obituary would have been more candid: "Yvonne, by her own hand, on November 29." And everyone would have gasped in horror. "To die without last rites; to kill and go to one's grave without confession! Skip over purgatory. Do not pass go. Do not collect $200. Go straight to jail. Go straight to hell." The emotional pain of that survivor, mother or father, wife or husband, child was forgotten. People acted as though nothing had happened; they didn't talk about the unspeakable. The whole sordid mess was hidden in the closet. In the twentieth century, gays creep out of the closet; death, especially suicide, we push back in, hiding it with all the other unmentionable skeletons.

Perhaps the day will yet come when newspapers will no longer carry death notices. They've already pared them down to little squares of dull data. Only the famous and infamous receive real obituaries. We can anticipate that by the year 2000 the tabloids will print in their finest typeface merely a list of names under the legal notices with all the tax sales and sheriff's auctions. Or perhaps by then a touch of a key on the ubiquitous home computer will provide an instant green readout of all those who have left this programmed life.

No matter, death is with me in a very real and overpowering way. It dogs me like a tired Labrador Retriever, rubbing against my thigh, tripping over my feet. It sprawls itself out on the middle of the floor, the most obvious object in the room. I must learn to accept this constant presence and all its nuances. I must welcome my own dying and the death of my dearest friends, the departure of my most precious love. Only then, when I have received it as a genuine part of life's complete journey, will I be able to keep walking, not in circles, but to some genuine destiny.

2

When All Seems Lost

You have hid your face from us.
Isaiah

Let me be gathered to the quiet west,
The sundown splendid and serene,
Death.
William Ernest Henley

I went to church the first Sunday in Advent. As a pastor I don't often just "go" to church, except occasionally when I'm away on vacation. When I do, I often grow restless, I fidget and fuss, waiting for the preacher to get to the point or the sky to split open. I often leave those vacationland houses of worship feeling that I wasn't privy to whatever agenda was hidden behind the blue-haired soprano belting out the anthem, or the invisible, but all-powerful board member quietly overseeing all the performances. Too often the energy is directed inward, rather than upward—or wherever God happens to be at the moment. At those times, going to church is like entering some spiritual black hole that sucks your body and soul into something you didn't intend but have no power to stop once started; and once alerted, you too become a part of that religious space that sucks everyone else in.

If we confess our sins God is just to forgive our sins and cleanse us from all unrighteousness.

So I go to church because I belong there; there is no better reason. In a manner of speaking, it's my turf; I'm the maestro, the master of ceremonies, the choreographer of the Sunday event, week after week. I am the one the hungry sheep usually look to, hoping to find a mouthful of grass they can taste and chew. They expect me, their pastor, to lead them to the cool refreshing waters of God's infinite goodness. But today I went to church because I want to find God for myself.

My two daughters and I sit in the pew as all respectable pew-sitters do, listening to lessons and prayers and long sermons, hearing above the voices the rustle of peppermint wrappers and the awful beating of our hearts in our aching breasts. I hear yesterday's words from the Office for the Burial of the Dead: "our departed sister." We hear our own helpless souls cry out for sweetheart and wife, for mother and friend. We want to muffle all the noises and at the same time break the deadening silence.

In Communion we pass the store-bought, enriched flour, preservative-laced, snow-white bread and sip Welch's grape juice from plastic throw-away glasses. We taste the sacra-

ment of death—a part of us irretrievably dead—and savor
the preserving salt of our river of tears. She is gone, and the
door is slammed shut so hard that all the mirrors of our
dreams have fallen from the walls, smashed into a million
shards of bad luck.

This is my body broken for you.

I glance at the service bulletin but it tells me nothing about
today's worship. The lessons were my lessons, and the sermon title was for the one I expected to preach. She probably
would have liked it; she most often did enjoy my preaching.
She was my front line critic, sometimes letting me know that
I had fallen flat on my face. More often, after I left the pulpit
feeling drained, her response would quickly return me to a
sense of self-worth. She had a way of getting me started
again.

The lections for the day included a passage from Isaiah 64:
"O that thou wouldst rend the heavens and come down ...
thou hast hid thy face from us ... we are the clay, you are the
potter." My sermon would be called "Murmurings to a Lost
God." I have yet to preach that sermon, yet in many ways I
have lived it out. Perhaps that kind is the most eloquent
preaching anyone can do.

I am thinking of death as we remember Christ's death. But
I am thinking more of hers. The thought of death is really the
first and the last of all our thinking. One thinks the worst
even while clinging to hopes for the best. I knew after she
had been missing that whole night, she would be dead; yet
after putting the pieces together in the morning, discovering

her car at our vacation cottage, I made the long trip without letting myself admit the possibility of her dying. A police officer greeted me there with, "I've got bad news," but I had to ask him twice before the awful truth sank in. Then the hammer, that seemed for those eternal seconds to hang in the space above me, was loosed and fell upon me with a thundering crash. All I can remember saying through gut-wrenching sobs was, "O God. She's gone. No. No."

"O God." God is the one who gets lost in our wishing and dreaming. Life as we know it, that familiar, fits-like-an-old-shoe routine, is supposed to go on and on. Nothing should change it. It can never stop, yet it always does. We talk about death in our creeds but in our daily grind we pretty much proclaim some kind of immortality. Then death strikes like that hammer blow, and the agony of grief sets in to stay a long time.

Now, years later as I write, my sorrow has slowed down like some worn-out wind-up tin drummer boy. Sadness fades like an old print; grief yields the right-of-way to my getting on with life; a semblance of promise paints a rosy blush on the distant horizon. Nevertheless, like a pile of nuclear waste, the tragic and painful episode will never altogether go away. In a given amount of time a huge fraction of the fallout of death will tick off into a distant memory; in another time increment an additional fraction of that remaining pain will be lost. There will always remain, though, a trace that stains the recesses of my mind. It will never be completely erased. It will never really let me go.

Neither will the feelings and impresssions I've expressed here ever end. To claim that all is now resolved, that my sorrow has passed away with the morning fogs, that every stab of pain is behind me for good, would be deceitful, foolish.

One part of the story, ended or not, lingers on and its effects hold to me with tenacious power: the way she went. Her self-destruction made my grief so much more soul-numbing, called me to such deep soul-searching. I bow to its uncomfortable consequence. I shall never know *why*, yet I will never stop asking.

As I look back at her life I see a single cord, woven of three strands, stitching together the dazzling patchwork quilt of her life signs and signals. These are only guesses, not certainties, facts that are difficult to interpret, but their pattern and its substance help satisfy my curiosity and relieve my anguish.

Her vocational death constitutes the first strand of that cord. Having felt truly called to her teaching profession, my wife made it her singular commitment, often putting all her emotional eggs in that one basket. From the warm roosts and hen houses of her classrooms she derived her deepest satisfaction. There she fortified her fragile ego, there she built her self-esteem, and there she found her primary reason for living. Her work was so much more than a job.

Sadly, in our technological, impersonal, and avaricious consumer society, people merely hold on to jobs. They put in their time, leave at the five o'clock bell, pick up their pay checks, and leave the whole business behind them. Work, for so many, becomes a necessary evil. They go at it grudgingly, at best resignedly. It is hard to fault them; the stressful conditions and uncertainty under which so many workers labor force them into an adversarial relationship with their occupations and employers.

Yvonne, on the other hand, refused to play that game. She enjoyed her work no matter how difficult and trying it became. She lived to influence and nurture her students, to celebrate her subject matter. The classroom yielded her greatest joys; it became a wellspring of deep satisfaction.

A walk into her classroom would have convinced anyone. Living plants hung from steampipes and lined the window sills, spreading out into the aisles. Animals frequently shared the greenhouse jungle: mice, hamsters, rabbits, gray squirrels, bright green snakes, a noisy crow, an inscrutable screech owl, bats. She covered walls and tack boards with signs of the seasons, illustrations, charts of scientific facts and curiosities. Her laboratory table was an arena for exciting demonstrations and exacting experiments. She peppered her presentations with amusing anecdotes; she encouraged laughter. She hugged six-foot athletes, kissed little boys on the head, embraced even the most difficult student with affection. In spite of all the fun and laughter, she always insisted on discipline, and the school administration entrusted to her their most obstreperous students. More than once she stepped between two football players to break up a fist-fight. Weighing only 100 pounds, she was known to march 200 pounders to the principal's office.

A spouse will boast like this, of course. My information comes from her colleagues, however, and can be substantiated by the numerous evaluations completed by her supervisors. Without exception they applauded her teaching skills, conduct, mastery of subject matter, ability to communicate facts and values, and commitment.

I also received my impressions directly from her. She laced our dinner hour with enthusiastic reports of her school days. Too often I listened with only one ear, but that never kept her from bubbling over with the joys and excitements, or bewailing the disappointments. She had little patience with the incompetence or indifference of other professionals; she smarted from the stupidity and cupidity of schoolhouse politics.

She was often over-conscientious, a perfectionist in scoring every paper and recording every grade. Not trusting her own subjective judgments, she would tally up every student's grades on a calculator to derive a precise numerical score upon which to base the final grade. She believed in a just return for every effort.

It came to an end too soon. For so great an investment of energy and skill, her career was far too short. After being dismissed the third consecutive year due to "reduction in force"—allegedly because of declining enrollment—she declared her career was over. It was gone, and with it her deepest life motivation. She threw out many of her plants—a radical move for someone who couldn't bear to thin out a row of zinnias. She packed her books, notes, lab exercises, quizzes, and equipment in corrugated boxes in a dark corner of the basement. They lie there to this day as though waiting to incubate some fresh, lively classroom experiment.

But the signals were sparse and subtle. In her last year she began divesting herself of those details that reinforced most strongly what ego she had left. When her sense of vocation trickled away, the life-blood drained out of her soul.

Whatever constitutes the bulk of grief, it comes in nauseating waves, the kind that lift a fishing boat to a crest and then suck it down into a trough with a sickening crash. At one moment we are left wrestling with the unreality of what is all too painfully real. That, I believe, is the initial blow of grief—unbelief. Death makes our real, believable life stand still like one frozen frame in an action scene. It leaves us and everything around us suspended in some ghostly space. It can't be true. But if it isn't true, then nothing is true, and only the unbelievable is true. We are stuck with that.

That she was gone seemed so unbelievable; time alone is painfully impressing me with that undeniable fact. "She's gone." I tried to convince myself, not so much of death as of departure. Death at its moment of intrusion is far too abstract to deal with. I am watching the train pull out of the station, watching the two faint, red lights on the last car disappear into the distance. I stand forlornly on the platform all alone. She's gone.

It is that wrenching away of her presence, that spatial separateness that haunts me now—even after these many months. I am denied the nearness of that particular person whose very closeness constituted a fundamental and essential part of my own life. It reminds me of Martin Buber's "I and Thou"—at least as I understand it. Without the *Thou* there can be no *I*. After thirty years of my being reflected in her person it is ontologically untenable for me to exist without her being at my side. I am not so lonely as I am alone. That is the grief I carry.

She mirrored well my own unique personhood, my idiosyncrasies; she had a special way of affirming the trifles of my daily experience. This is what I miss: that one person with whom I can share the most trivial event. We could bounce off one another simply unimportant information and always receive some kind of acknowledgment. Our lives, though small, never went unnoticed. Now that source of knowledge and my awareness of being myself is gone. The tiny gems and germs that make up my life fall and scatter, getting lost in all the cracks of this huge world.

Outlasting the initial shock and trauma of unbelief, the tremors and feelings of separation persist. As the first aspect of grief or reaction to death wore off, and her dying became a believable fact in history, the sense of departure—the goneness—dug in all the more deeply. I began to notice this about three weeks after her death. Something in my emotional make-up had turned around. I became more active, began to make some stabs at pastoral work, busied myself with a host of financial and legal matters that have a habit of presenting themselves at the loss of a family member. I went to the YMCA for a swim, walked the dog, completed an unfinished Christmas project for my daughter. I started to eat full meals and regularly cook for myself. But such heartening signs don't often last long for me; another wave breaks on the shore and sweeps me off my feet.

Early on the fourth Sunday in Advent I drove alone to that cemetery where we had laid her to rest. The sun had just begun to cast its long shadows on the frosty ground. The horizontal light accented a portion of the text encircling the rotunda that stood like a lone sentinel on the flat landscape: "...all ye that labor ...." The rest of the verse circled around the other side, out of sight. My drive that morning through the park-like burial ground became a kind of mystical pilgrimage as I approached her grave. Floral blankets were spread across acre upon acre; here and there were more sensational decorations: completely trimmed Christmas trees, mylar balloons twisting in the air on their tethers, foil pinwheels, a plastic cross striped like a candy cane. I walked quietly across the bare space, passing grave after grave, marker after marker, leaving blackish prints in the frozen grass as my feet metered the distance to that hallowed spot.

Thousands of graves, each bearing silent testimony to grief such as mine, surrounded me. I was not alone, yet in my thoughts I was terribly alone. There were no sounds, no voices. Only the chill ground and the icy sod. A trickle of other devoted souls came into view, while a trickle of tears ran down my face. I was overcome by a sense of desolation, a haunting reminder that I would never see her again.

She is gone. Death always comes in the past perfect tense. The action is completed, over and done. And I am alone, desperately alone. The initial shock and stunning unbelief are giving way to the deep abiding sorrow of absence.

Again we were in church to hear carols, lessons, a sermon, idle chatter, and the rustle of peppermint wrappers. I left feeling as empty as when I entered. People reached out painfully to show their care, belying their frustration: How do you comfort your pastor? They were as dumbstruck as the neighbors of Job. I pitied them; I loved them. But God didn't break this long silence of mine; he spoke through no one. His Word didn't carry with it the force it once had in my heart. It either went over my head, getting lost in the busy noise around me, or it simply wasn't there. The silence of God is a part of my sorrow.

In his letters from prison, Dietrich Bonhoffer speaks about such separation and reasons that only wishful thinking expects God to fill the void left by a loved one's departure. No, God leaves the heart vacant so that we feel all the more acutely what we have lost. In the deepest sense we lose ourselves. Grief knows that for us to survive we must take on a new identity—a formidable task.

Taking on a new me is fraught with dangers as well as difficulty; only a dangerous conceit believes my "I" can out-survive hers, that it can go on in spite of her. That kind of conceit makes my survival through this grief an arrogant enterprise, yet I have no choice but to survive. The options surface only as an unanswerable rhetorical question: *Why couldn't it have been me?* And here I am not revealing my altruism but my fear and cowardice. We are afraid to live the life that is uniquely our own. At least I am.

Grief recognizes this as one side of the coin: "I am all alone." The other side is equally true: "You have no choice; you must go on and live from here no matter how painfully uncertain, no matter how undesirable, how impossible." Death calls us to this. Whatever else sorrow does to me, it always brings me back to my senses. Every sound, small object, trifle, trigger the over-arching feelings that invade life. Where depression leaves me destitute of feeling, numb and empty as a vacuum of the spirit, sorrow comes at me with too much feeling, a mountain of pain, a saturation of hurt. It picks up signals all around me: articles of clothing, a visit to the grocery store, house plants, a shelf of books, Christmas gifts never wrapped, dog hair swept from the floor, ripe pears on the kitchen table, Milky Way candy bars, pictures of her hauntingly beautiful face. The comforts of friends, of grown men weeping, a church overflowing in our

20

memorial tribute to her, all fill me and choke me with sorrow and tears. Most of all I see what could have been. I want to shout: "You could have made it. Life was not that bad!" I feel for her as my poor baby who couldn't hold on to life's crack-the-whip played on this frozen pond. In the crazy corners of my mind I hear myself talk: "My dear, I miss you. I loved you. How I wish I'd known more and done more. How happy we could have been together."

But she's gone.

It's all over, and all the talk is academic. Sorrow cuts into the soul like a jabbing, piercing sword, the *coup de grace*. Death strikes with an all-or-nothing finality; it is the non-negotiable transaction that no one barters for; it is the finish of all finishes. That stunning, shuddering, incontrovertible fact pushes us around as a cat does a mouse. Death doesn't listen to reason, hears no cries for mercy, knows no pity. Sorrow is our only response to its ugly and persistent pressure, our feeble effort to keep living and somehow justify the agony, to understand the unfathomable and senseless.

We live in a sensate world. We smell the fresh-mown grass and the fields scattered with cow manure. We taste watermelon and garlic and fine old wine. We hear babies cry and crickets chirp and choirs sing Bach's "Magnificat." We touch the bark of trees, the cold face of coins hidden in our pockets, the hair and skin and shape of the person we love. The world is a catalog for the senses; my life is that particular collection of sensory experiences that are uniquely mine. Take the bread, feel its soft and crumbly texture, smell it fresh from the oven, hear it munched on by the hungry, taste its sweetness. "This is my body broken for you." Listen as the liquid wine pours from the bottle, look at its claret brilliance, smell the heady aroma, taste the sweet bitterness, feel its first touch on your lips. "My blood shed for you."

Death, however, defies the senses and leaves a hole in the fabric of our nicely-reasoned, well-structured, law-abiding universe. You can handle a dead body but you really can't touch death. The battlefield lingers with the so-called smell of death—really the stench of the abandoned dead—for death itself has no smell; it is too intangible to apprehend with any of the senses. We can approach it no more clearly than we can see the space within the atom, or taste the key of B flat minor, or hear the color green, or catch the wind and map its texture. Though I may have the touch of a blind musician, the ear of an owl, the eye of an eagle, the tongue of a wine taster, the nose of a bird dog, death is out of reach, senseless. It is that senselessness that multiplies the already crippling ache.

To call death senseless is not to assert that it's meaningless. Death has meaning, I suppose; at least we attribute meaning to it. Theologians have done so for centuries; hollow piety continues to announce with assurance what death and deaths mean: "It's all for the best." "It's the Lord's will." We may lend death meaning through the wisdom of biology, evolution, or the second law of thermodynamics. Perhaps my wife's death was for the best; just don't tell me that.

22

Maybe the genetic pool is being refined and perfected as each generation comes and goes. Believe, if you will, something good will come of my disaster. But death's endless stillness won't budge, it will not respond. It remains that awful senseless last page of a whole dictionary of meanings. It strikes the living as an affront to their senses.

I am tempted to discover miracles worked by her death. But they are mostly delusions and really add no significance to her dying. Crowds could have thronged our little church without this nightmare; friends could have come to my side; people could have made claims as eloquent about their faith as they did after her memorial service; and I could have been just as close to my daughters without my wife's death. If her death has any meaning it is locked up somewhere in her grave as are all the deaths reported in the Old Testament. The secrets are asleep, hidden in Sheol.

My daughters and I went to the fresh, week-old grave to lay a blanket of hemlock, pine cones and satin ribbons on the freshly dug earth. We paused to collect our thoughts and feelings, feelings that seemed to evade us. We were numb; the grave would not speak (it never does; it remains silent and still as the thousands of others around us lie mute). But the silence clearly revealed to us that all of life, with all its marvelous sensations and reactions, really comes down to this: In death we seem more at one with the whole than in life. All that makes us unique seems to vanish. We are all bound together in the same dust and clay.

23

Grief asks: "What does this mean?" It hears no answer.

There I struggle, with that darkest, deepest dimension of my loss. The senselessness of death seems so easily to slip into the senselessness of life. The line between the two is as fine as gossamer, and we too smoothly cross into that dangerous nihilistic darkness.

A week earlier, on this very piece of earth, we recited the Creed together. "He descended into hell." The sun shone warmly on that first day of December, although the ubiquitous funeral tent shielded us from its radiance. Credo ... He descended into hell. That God should go where God is not, where God can't possibly be? This unresolvable paradox is my grief; and yet here I finally understand death. It is that moment when God is lost, and to him I murmur and cry.

As the text for the first Sunday in Advent speaks: "You have forsaken us." You, God, have forsaken us in your descent to hell; and in that moment, this fantasy of life and this playpen world have become that hell. Here we touch the center of sorrow.

3

The Wilderness

John was clothed with camel's hair,
and he had a leather girdle around his waist,
and ate locusts and wild honey.
And he preached ...
"Prepare the way of the Lord"
St. Mark

There were lions all around him ...
a lot closer than I'd ever seen a man
and a lion before ...
Frederick Buechner in *Lion Country*

John, in the wilderness, the recluse, the hermit, probably talked to himself like a crazy man. The wilderness does that even to sane men.

Not that John wasn't sane, too sane for the rest of his world, and his being out of step with the rest of the priests, scribes, bigots, Herodians, Philistines, and Pharisees was what made his the only voice worth hearing. Noises abounded, but the messages came through garbled.

25

The voices and noises around us produce the same effect.

Politicians smile or rant, promise or scowl. But they are so often hollow sounding gongs, hammers on spent oil drums.

Show business parades before an incredulous public its shallow wisdom; and the naive grovel and claw their way to see and hear the latest gossip—the hot air of talk shows and tabloid newspapers.

I am thinking of John and Advent as the Christmas story comes to me through the electronic nasal-pharynx of Perry Como from scratchy Japanese record players. A host of pompous preachers puff themselves up with unctuous sounds. The air waves vibrate with their garbled words and diluted messages.

I would preach on John the Baptist on that second Advent Sunday—the man who was out of step. I myself would have to feel out of step to do it; and I would dare the sheep to walk out of step to all the mindless throngs at the shopping malls and office parties. To prepare the way is to break file, to march to a new beat, to sing in a different key. Not many venture to that wilderness place. Not many bow under the water of the spirit. Not many can leave their yule log comfort and soak themselves in the Jordan.

People who do, who wander in a winter desert, talk to themselves.

Grief makes us wander there, causes us to take un-measured steps, sing out of tune. I may not talk aloud—al-though at times I do—but I find myself so often talking to myself like that desert hermit. The spoken word, the thought-

26

through word, comes garbled through the deep sobs and flood of tears; but it always wants to be heard. I speak to myself in the mirror and watch the water from my blurred eyes wash down the lather before the blade scrapes my skin. I argue with myself when I fight to sleep at night; when I awake I must remind myself, "You are alone here. There is no one else in this bed." I dictate the directions that need to be spelled out in my disorganized brain. Behind the wheel of the car, next to the washer, in front of the sink as I tidy up a few dishes.

I knew clearly for months that Yvonne was going through torment and anguish. Her emotions moved between worry and anxiety into rage and depression. How much stress was hers to handle, and how deep her capacity for distress, was only a guess. Suffering is such a personal experience; we can't appreciate how one reacts differently to given painful stimuli as compared to another. My hunch is that either her emotional burden was beginning to paralyze her, or that something of organic origin was affecting her.

She increasingly worried about the latter. Six years prior to Yvonne's death, her mother died in the advanced stages of Alzheimer's Disease. Though today it is a widely publicized affliction treated in numerous household journals, television and popularized medical reporting, Alzheimer's was hardly known to the general public when her mother, at a relatively early age, began to manifest its symptoms. Never content with meager knowledge, Yvonne thoroughly researched the subject, learning more and more along with others in her family, since an aunt and uncle were also diagnosed to have this condition. Perhaps that little knowledge became a dangerous thing, for a few years ago she became convinced she too was falling prey to Alzheimer's.

Only she could have possibly known how frequent or serious were her lapses of memory, her inability to perform simple mechanical tasks, her frustation with speech. Frequently, however, when facing such a difficulty, she would cry out: "I'm going crazy!" or she would attempt to explain away unusual behavior with, "I can't help it. I have Alzheimer's." Perhaps it was true.

Once a gifted public speaker, her speech became alarmingly disorganized. She would misplace her handbag or lose her keys—an entirely new and bizarre behavior pattern for the rest of us to witness. Burning pots and pans, mistiming a dinner, were noticeable, but tiny annoyances. Her recent entry into the business world brought her face-to-face with new frustrations. Although a skilled typist and efficient organizer, she encountered unusual difficulty with office tasks: steno, typing, operating a calculator. On several occasions she walked off the job in the middle of the day, convinced she was a failure. She complained about the difficulties she had with tasks which others would take in stride. These patterns are often typical and associated with Alzheimer's. Whether these were early symptoms or continuing manifestations of deepening anxiety, we can never know.

Grief is a noisy business, even when we keep our mouths closed and our tongues still. Like so many free shots in a pinball game, our thoughts and questions echo around in the hollow of our skulls. Tiring work, grief toils to express itself, verbalizing even to the inner self.

The hard work, however, has its rewards. I find the payoff comes, not so much when I am babbling to myself, but when I am free to talk to others, to let out all the stops of the full range of my feelings. That would happen during those early days following her death and would trickle along in the weeks that trailed after that. My friends and her friends; my family and her relatives, members of my daughter's circles, all came into my life in those few days, and all evoked from me my grief talk.

Perhaps I've learned to be more open with feelings than most others, for the talk came freely, and the catharsis felt better than silence. Somehow my talk put the horrified and speechless at ease. I found myself reaching out to those I loved and who loved her. They, too, were hurting and it surprised me to discover this role switch: I was consoling my consolers.

We are verbal creatures. *Homo sapiens*, the thinking man, could just as well deserve the Linnaen name *Homo dicens*, the talking man. At his best and at his worst he speaks. On his mountaintops he shouts at the top of his lungs hoping that Echo will approve. In the dark valleys he whispers, hoping against hope he is not alone. When honored, he stands up to make a speech; in his sorrow he is expected to talk. And he does.

The police officer, at that first shocking moment, expected me to talk. "I know this is hard for you," and "I am very sorry, but can you answer a few questions?" He was only doing his job, but it seemed too obvious to me that I had no answers. I should be asking the questions! The questions, the Big Questions, were mine to ask!

The mortician expected me to talk that afternoon, to talk reasonably. And the bankers. And then all the callers, visitors, understandably dumb comforters. I needed to speak with them all: "How are you?" "Oh, just fine, thank you." "How are you doing?" "Just beautifully." "What can I do for you? "A cold beer would be nice." I didn't always say what I wanted to say but found myself second guessing the needs of my comforters. I should prefer to have said something quite different: "What can you do for me? You can bring her back from the dead! Or you can bawl your fool head off as I am. Or you can just stand there like a dumb ass, or, better still, say something wise like Balaam's ass." "How am I?" "How do I feel?" "Absolutely rotten, if you really have to know."

So I talk on and on to whoever will listen to my sense and nonsense, my resignation and my rancor. It washes me out; I feel better, but not well.

"John was in the wilderness preaching, the kingdom of God is at hand." I would too someday be preaching again, but for then they were just words. The Word creates. The Word destroys. The Word becomes flesh and lives among the dying. The words wash us and make us clean and new. So I talk: to you, to myself in my wild desert, but mostly I talk to her.

I don't talk to those waxy remains doctored up for display in the funeral chapel. I leave that to the hysterical who need to be seen rather than heard, and I need to be heard. That shell of a once vivacious woman I knew and loved couldn't hear me no matter how loudly I screamed. That all too dead, ghastly, stranger's face lying on the brocade pillow had only a passing resemblance to the one I kissed good-bye that last morning. Bodies "laid out" say little to me, and I can say nothing to them. But in my own irrational way I talk to her as though she has to be told and I'm the only one who can tell her. So I've been talking to her day and night.

"Where are you tonight, my love? I am so worried. Our daughter paces the floor; I stare out the window at midnight's hopeless blackness and see nothing. We waited all through the night, searched the parking lots, looked for your car, called around. Nothing. Friends came by in the morning. I called your office and learned that you left at 12:30, just after noon. You never kept your doctor's appointment, nor did you go shopping. You kept your dark secret so well.

"I shall relive that scene a thousand times, my dear. Our neighbor at the cottage, Mary Ann, found you. Brother Bo drove me to our lake house. I lost you.

"We drove up our lane to be greeted by a crowd of policemen. My mind knew but my heart held back. 'Did she do it?' I asked. (IT should be spelled out in capital letters; so tiny a word stands for the enormity of the act.) 'Yes,' he replied. I saw the pill vial in his hand. We walked to the front door through the little house you loved so much, into your special glassed-in room. 'Is she gone?' I needed to fortify what I already knew. When he answered again, all the lights of my world went out. I want you to know how sick I felt, what terror paralyzed me, what painful tears erupted, how devastated your death left me.

"I gazed, as though it were the last time, out the big glass door across your deck, and let my stricken eyes sweep across our woodland yard. A late November frost had left your garden gray, stiff, still. Not a bird came to our feeders; branches of the trees you and I planted hung silently in the quiet winter air. They took your little body away, and we drove home to the longest day.

"You should know how grown men cried like babies when they heard the news, when they came to see me. Friday night was an endless procession of family and friends. Flowers, fruit, calls, memorial gifts came from all over. I don't blame you for the hurt, dear, but I have never known such pain in all my life. As with David, my tears are my meat day and night. If every crevice in me is filled with choking grief, I think how wretched and awful *your* pain must have been.

"Saturday arrived, the day to say our final 'Good-bye.' My clergy friends led us in a brief prayer and burial service. It was simple and to the point as you would have preferred. We wept openly at the open grave and throughout the day that seemed to have closed off all our dreams. On Sunday night we remembered you with solid, majestic hymns like 'I Greet Thee Who My Great Redeemer Art,' a brass quintet played Bach's 'Little Fugue' and 'Sleepers, Wake!'—the Word of God. The church was overflowing and that brought me a kind of contentment in the midst of so much sorrow. We greeted people and embraced: your friends from two schools, the lake, the church, the Board on which you served, the church at large, of course family and neighbors and friends. If only you knew how many loved and admired you—would that have changed your mind?

"You are resting now. This is what you wanted for a long time, isn't it? How often I've seen you escape from the stresses of your life, and from the fatigue of work to which you gave so much of yourself, by crawling early into your bed, fashioning around you a cocoon of covers. Sleep was one of your most precious quests. And now it's forever yours. O, sweet Morpheus. If you were not the Christian you were, I should think that Morpheus might have been your patron. It was fitting that he should wrap you up in a blanket and carry you away from all time. Sleep well, my baby, my sweet one."

Weariness, sleeplessness, and exhaustion take their toll on grief, bad enough as it is in itself. On occasions I would be overtaken by a few winks of sleep, a few good hours. But rest would come slowly and I would wake early. When resurrected to the early morning darkness, she was never there. The truth was so heartless, the loss so heavy a burden, the sorrow such brutally difficult work. I was left spent; and in my restless tossing, in the middle of the night, she came to me—in my wild dreams. And there she seemed to speak to me.

As I lay weeping, she appeared, put her arms around me to comfort me. It was just like those times she spent long hours at my hospital bedside, encouraging me, nursing me, nurturing me with her strengths, back to health. I heard her say in the reverie: "It will be all right." I know, however, the dead don't speak; it was only a dream and she was only a mysterious, unreal, Mona Lisa presence.

Yet in those dreams, occurring almost every night in those early weeks, I seemed to find some way to hold on to her. That holding made the parting less implacable, less insane. Even the absurd visions in my brief sleep brought me back to some level of companionship. In that wilderness, I could keep talking:

"I dream of your loving me—one night of our wrestling as we did when we were young and joyfully foolish. Our pas-

sion and laughter mingled together like the colors of the
rainbow. Then the whole scene was gone. On another night
we rolled off the deck of an old house—whose it was I'll
never know—and had to make a hasty retreat indoors. But
we were unembarrassed and innocent. Last night you arrived
as a dead ringer for Sargent's mystery woman in that in-
famously famous painting. Your gown, however, had narrow
straps supporting the low-cut bodice—straps which I began
to pull down.

"As in my dreams, so in my life there is a lot of wishing
and contemplation. It is like my Christmas shopping for your
grown daughters who, at this time of year, are still little girls.
You were too. Before you left me, I had been busy lining up
some gifts that would please my fancy, and, I hoped, yours
too. I bought Debbie some records of the Baroque period,
and Beth a book on Van Gogh, and some other odds and ends
that I have forgotten since the bleak passage of Christmas. I
wanted to get you some nice clothes—something I haven't
done for a few years since our tastes began to spread apart.
You were going in for more and more 'work wear' which to
me looked too dowdy and drab. This year the fashions are
off-the-wall, high style, all glitter. I focused on some smart
wool suits, fit for an executive, for you. I would, however,
have preferred to have bought you one of those ridiculous
party dresses—something flashy, sequined, brazen, sexy.
Since we go to no parties nor hang out at bars, you would
have positively no use for it. Except to look great. I was
selfish with you and I still am. I hunger for the way you

"turned me on." You belong next to me, arousing my animal desires and feelings. I think of you close to me, offering courage, lending me support, evoking the man in me. Now you are gone; I must learn to walk alone and sleep alone and dream alone."

My tales and stories, rambling though they are, do not partake of superstition or magic. Through this desert talk I draw as close as I can possibly get, in this sorrow, to prayer. I talk to myself like a mad man, to my friends I babble on, to my love I murmur under my breath. Yet in all of this I talk with God. Like smoke and incense from the altar of my grief, the verbal stuff of my agony rises upward to him as a sweet smelling offering.

"John was in the wilderness preaching … the axe is laid to the root of the tree …He shall baptize you with fire." In these weeks I have not preached that sermon on John, but I have lived out the Word; I've been touched by the fire; the axe has bitten into my roots; I have walked with the Lamb of God.

4

Memory

Do this in remembrance of me.
St. Luke

Memory! You have the key.
T.S. Eliot

The liturgy read: "This supper is a feast of remembrance, of communion and of hope." It embraces the three tenses of our salvation. We are vindicated only in God's past; we are sanctified in the fires that burn in the present; our glory is all promise: tomorrow.

My grief is that I have tomorrow on my mind. I fear to walk those steps, those roads, those miles alone. I loathe the thought of the future being so different. That one little moment—her dying moment—has wrenched from my hand the last reflexive grip I've had on my own fate. Like a slide show, one click and the whole picture changes.

37

Well-meaning friends tell me I'll cherish good memories, and I've told hundreds of mourners the same. Perhaps some day I shall. But for now, in this pain, this grief, my memories mean so little to me. They don't reach out to console, they don't brighten that gloomy horizon, they don't line with gold the poverty of my soul. I long for a better tomorrow—that's foremost on my mind. I am waiting for the day she will come out of her fears and doubts, when she will finally affirm the goodness of life, when she will once again radiate that joy that had been so often, so clearly, hers.

We had begun making bold plans for our older years: we would travel to the ends of the continent, soak in the desert sun, stand in the green mists of the Pacific Northwest, smell the good earth of the Great Plains once again, explore the dark corners of southern swamps, perhaps reach as far as Alaska. We would watch grandchildren grow and plot their years, enjoying every stage in their development. We'd mostly watch daffodils bloom, springtime arrive, fish splash and summer's lightning flash. We should sit in the shade of the trees we planted and slice fat tomatoes and watch a thousand autumn sunsets. We would live fully every day God would give us.

The longing lingers, making me feel so acutely how I want her at my side at the rim of the Grand Canyon or in a small pub in San Francisco. I want her to share with me the warmth of a gentler climate, and in the warmth around the Christmas tree where our littlest grandbaby plays and sings. She will not be there. All I have left are memories; that's what stings.

During the Advent season, our memory plays tug-of-war with longing. Yesterday pulls with all its might against tomorrow. My loss has left me hanging on those taut cords, dangling on this stretched-out present—this hollow day that won't go away—which is like an instrument strung with cat gut strung between yesterday and the future. I pluck on it a discordant tune.

In that awful gnawing ache I must be sensing the desire of the prophets who had at least an inkling of the far-off Messiah. They reach out for the unreachable. Like today's Jew, they have a better appreciation of this season we call Advent than we Christians have. We sometimes really believe we have the future all wrapped up, addressed, delivered. It's always Christmas for us. We never have to wait. The Jew, on the other hand, has no Christmas; he waits and weeps for the Messiah who delays too long. He falls back on his remembrances of Moses, Abraham, David. Their story is a yearning for the presence of the Lord like that of Job, Jeremiah, the prophets of the exile. It is our story, too, our waiting for his appearance; we tell it again and again in the Lord's Supper. "Do this in remembrance of me ... till I come." It is in this present moment—in this my grief-stricken today—against the backdrop of yesterday's memories that I must wait for the sun to rise tomorrow.

I watch the sun set and remain below the horizon, giving only a teasing hint of its power with winter's long, grotesque shadows and short days. The darkened streets are warm with the glow of strings of twinkling lights, flashing stars, luminous crèches. But for me it is still dark and all that my mind can pull up from the past week, the events surrounding her death, the shock and unbelief in those fleeting moments that followed. Memories:

Thursday: It repeats in my mind like the tick-tock of the old school house clock. I choke for breath with each telephone call I make. We order funeral and flowers. The house spills over with family and friends. Her sister arrives at midnight. The following hours bring no sleep.

Friday: The air stings with cold; my pain is sharper still. I'm hungry but cannot eat. I search for the cemetery deed. I greet scores at the "viewing."

Saturday. The last "good-bye" comes so soon and yet not soon enough. We assemble at ten in the morning. The weather is good for weeping. We ride silently in the limousine, each holding his and her own thoughts. Perhaps we have no thoughts to share; they're buried as well. A bare-chested he-man sells cigarettes from the roadside billboard; spray-paint graffiti spells "cancer" across his tanned skin. I go home to eat yogurt and jello and play for a moment with Becky, our first and only grandchild—mine alone now.

Sunday: We go to church and eat the Lord's Supper. We scurry out before the congregation does. It's more comfortable for us and for them. I sleep most of the afternoon. For brief moments my spirits are lifted by the Christian affirmations at the Memorial Service at night. The church is filled and spilling over. Everyone goes home, and then I am left exhausted, dry, worn-out from grief, from life as well as death. We try to sleep.

Monday: Piles of mail arrive. We open envelopes and pass sympathy cards around. The girls rummage through a box of old family pictures. We choose our favorite snapshots of their mother. Debbie's car is disabled on the highway. We get a tow-truck to haul it home. The driver assures us in his heavy accent: "I am Armeenian. I feex yourr carr. My mudder, she die too." We take her sister and husband to the airport and make a wish on the brilliant sunset.

Tuesday: I compose a tribute to my wife for inclusion in the acknowledgments we will send to all our friends. I go to the office and dump all the work on my secretary—can't concentrate. Some members of my family visit me tonight, breaking up an intolerably long and lonely period of time. Each day becomes an eon.

Wednesday: More of the same. Though my weeping is less frequent, I still have no energy. I think I am just cried out, for the pain is no less. We place a grave blanket on the freshly dug earth. Beth and I do some grocery shopping and spend a quiet night. We do not eat, nor do we sleep. The night is very long.

Thursday: A week has past. Only a week, but so drawn-out. Snow is on the ground when we rise. Crows swallow huge chunks of moldy bread spread on the side lawn. The snow melts quickly. We listen to our niece sing Christmas carols at the mall. I squeeze the tears back in, the first time I have held them back.

Friday: We rise late but as weary as ever. I open mail, answer more calls from around the country, pay bills, run errands. Kids on the walks are doing "wheelies" with their bikes. I pick at a frozen dinner that I don't feel like eating. Food is a stranger to me. We return home early from a book club meeting. The moon is full and bright.

Saturday: It is a week since we buried her! I can't believe what is happening. It all takes place around me and seemingly in spite of me. This reality with which I must deal seems to come from another dimension in space. I must have walked through some science fiction time warp. *Chronos* moves along; *kairos* stands motionless. Visitors drop in during the afternoon and say so little. Beth and I eat at the drive-in, then take a drive to watch the New York City skyline. Yvonne always enjoyed that view from our side of the river, from her Hoboken. Night falls upon us and seven million others in the big city. I have an awful cry before I go to bed.

Sunday: Church again, and more sobbing—mine and others'. The congregation offers more time for healing. They do their best in caring for me without stepping all over me. Family visitors in the afternoon bring dinner, and for once, we eat well. We watch television for the first time since she's been gone. Ironically, a painful reminder, a program dealing with Alzheimer's disease, and the brain.

Yvonne was convinced she was an early Alzheimer's victim. She asked me more than once to "put her away" when she became hopelessly demented. She persisted in demanding this promise from me—one that I could not possibly make. My daughter and mother relate similar incidents in which Yvonne vowed never to put us through the kind of anguish her father faced, or that any of us witnessed with her mother. She even suggested a divorce so I would be free to go on living.

Any response to such a proposition would have put me in an untenable position. If I had said yes, I would have had to violate all my marriage vows—promises I held sacred. I would stay with her, I insisted, no matter how prolonged and demanding the caregiving. Such care "till death us do part" is expected. Yet having said no, I wonder if I didn't fail to take seriously the covenant she sought to make.

That she would want a divorce under such circumstances could signal her desire to get out of our marriage, but her commitment to that marriage and her concern about her family's suffering in the event she would develop Alzheimer's mitigate against that notion.

The evidence about her condition hangs by an exceedingly thin thread, but, as with articles of faith and hope, we suspend from them a great deal of weight. Even though a clinical diagnosis is unavailable (and we shall never know) the fact that she took her life with this in mind, makes all the difference in the world. Her act, which suddenly plunged me into the darkest night I could imagine, may indeed have been precipitated by a desire to spare me years of gray and lifeless days.

I must confess that I want to believe she was right about her condition, that hers was a courageous deed, that this final act was one of the most responsible she could ever have done. As a clergyman friend said, "Under those circumstances that was a life-affirming act." Hendrikus Berkhof, the renowned Dutch theologian, responded to my question with this: "I would say she did that out of a sense of Christian responsibility." In *The Myth of Sysiphus*, Albert Camus states that suicide is perhaps the most creative act some people can ever come to do.

Camus also writes in the same book, "The greatest of all philosophical questions is raised by suicide: Is life worth living?" I don't believe Yvonne was seeking to answer any philosophical questions, and, although I believed from my perspective that even her life was worth living, she obviously, at least in one awful, decisive moment, did not. It seems to me that somehow she was destined to be tormented by life and its choices, as though the unseen demons were holding her in their bondage.

Our family physician, seeking to console me shortly after her death, offered the opinion that suicide is like a disease. Some people are afflicted by it and are destined to take their lives no matter how impulsive or implausible the act. Somewhere between the two, solving philosophical conundrums and yielding to the fates, the essence of my wife's death must lie. I could not deny that she was capable of suicide. She had mentioned it once before and confided to me that once she seriously planned it, but that was many years ago. Regardless, I could not tie her down or monitor her every move. She was a free human being and she lived and died accordingly. How free was this last act of hers is difficult to say.

After her death, my fleeting memories contain: limousines and bare-chested men smoking cigarettes, grave blankets, frozen dinners warmed up in a microwave, sympathy cards, church services with their peppermint wrappers shattering the stillness, wet handkerchiefs. I wonder if that is all that life will ever be from now on? How can we put such stock in memories?

The possibilities for calling up pleasant memories are virtually limitless. The human brain contains billions of neurons, nerve cells, each capable of reacting with another or of interacting in groups, each more complex than a microchip, each a potential safe deposit box for incoming data, information, stimuli. The good memories are there along with the bad, waiting to be sorted out. Storing memories and remembering, however, are two very different activities. Somehow one must be highly selective in the retrieval of data from this organic memory bank.

The facts, unfortunately, are not on our side, considering what science understands about the brain. Rarely can we go back into the glow of our past and pull out the single item we cherish. I can remember the many happy camping trips we've taken together. I can reach back to that warm, sweet feeling of snuggling together in a sleeping bag on a frosty morning. But specific mornings and trips are really lost in a past that has melted together over the years.

I want to remember all those thousands of times we made love together, yet, though each one was special, singular incidents are unavailable for recall, and I wouldn't tell if they were. Her coloratura soprano so often moved me; but what song other than Handel's "I Know That My Redeemer Liveth" or "Come Unto Me"? And what occasion? She loved Christmas and opening small gifts. I can visualize her looks of surprise, joy, or puzzlement on Christmas morning, but I can't connect them with any particular gift or any specific Christmas morning.

There are some of the "flash-bulb" events, as they are called, that I can remember: our first kiss, our wedding night, the way she looked at me after our daughters were born. I can recall her painful crying when I brought her the news of her mother's death; and her gloating laughter after she caught a twelve-pound bluefish when I had caught none. These come to the fore because our memory is enhanced by the emotion attending the event. The more intense the feelings the more accessible to the memory is the event. Few of us live lives so emotionally charged that we can truly, accurately retrieve all of it. Such a life would be painfully difficult. Often only our crisis events are preserved with strong emotions. For our own survival we can't forget them, and then we too easily forget the good stuff.

Memories fail me in this journey of grief precisely because those emotions—that constellation of feelings, frights, excitement—are locked up and therefore not so readily accessible as the images. Our history passes before us as a row of fleeting pictures, snapshots flipped with a thumb, passing in a blur before our eyes. The images are indeed precious; but the feelings of joy, security, enchantment, mystery, eros, anger, sorrow, peace, happiness all are absent from them. The bitter-sweet feelings that attend our recollections are really nostalgia, a diffuse, faceless form of feeling. What we gather in that recall process are reminiscences, not events.

And the present in which we struggle conditions the retrieval of the past. My present grief colors everything I see and think and remember. It paints my past thirty years with her in romantically rosy tones. It casts a soft back-light around her and her relationship with me. It is a glamorous portrait, real or not. Next to it, any possible future looks dismally gray, somberly ugly. Such a biased look back makes a look at the future a chore. I seem glued to this present moment, unable to budge, stunned by the force of such enormous events.

On the other hand, those feelings of the present—those domineering, nagging, annihilating feelings—not only color the dim, pastel emotions of yesteryear, they almost seem to erase them. They come forward like some dull lump. Numbness is the best word to describe the sensation of reaching back or ahead in the hour of death. The past week seems like an hour; the week before me looks like an eternity.

This do in remembrance of me.

The mystery of the sacrament, the wonder of God's grace, the presence of the Word make real the past. We believers come to the table with no memories as such of Jesus and his death. How then can we "remember his death till he comes"? Those remembrances are God's. Only he can make them ours. It is in our deliberate act of remembering—or trying to remember—that God's grace comes to us.

It is memory, not remembrance, that sustains me. Remembrances, unless creatively reconstructed as only a few artists can do, seal us in the past. Memory, on the other hand, is my contact with life, the light that directs me to accept my own existence, my pull toward tomorrow.

"Remember Jesus Christ risen from the dead," counsels St. Paul. In the resurrection God claims all the future as his own. The power to remember bridges the vast dark space that is my today, and ushers me into tomorrow.

A feast of remembrance, of communion, and of hope.

5

Wondering Why

We walk by faith, not by sight.
St. Paul

*'Twas grace that taught my heart to fear,
and grace my fears relieved.*
John Newton

If my longing for the future makes small the significance of
my recollections, even more so does my question "Why?" It
reduces all my certainties to dust and ashes. Since a child I
have needed to know why and how things work. That they
simply happen the way they do never satisfies my curiosity.
Now it goes beyond childlike curiosity, and there are no
all-wise grownups to give me answers.

Why? The persistent question makes my grief especially
acute, yet I believe it is a part of everyone's sorrow. We don't
receive answers we seek; school is out, and the homework

hasn't been handed in. We are left to wonder. We must live on, yet can't, without knowing for sure why.

As the days following her death wear down I feel my mind constantly inquiring about that decisive moment, that event, that feeling which led her to her act. Why did she do it? We can find no real, hard clues. All the circumstantial evidence points in another direction. The answer to my search lies somewhere hidden in her psyche, a self that was determined to hide itself from the world. As only I can fully know my grief, only she could fully know and appreciate the deep, painful secrets she carried around for so long.

I am neither inclined nor competent to analyze Yvonne's personality. Nevertheless, the stories she frequently told me about her childhood were significant. She wouldn't or couldn't let go of the past. She repeated her story so often that I would become impatient and uneasy. Through her tales, happy and sad, she must have been trying to say more; what she related fits too well the scheme suggested by Transactional Analysis regarding life scripts. Her losing life script and "don't be" injunctions are too important to dismiss out of hand.

In the summer of 1932, not far from the runways of the new airport and dreams for a modern world, in Newark, when sweltering heat lay like a quilt over Elizabeth, New Jersey and the dark depression dragged at the heels of laborers and merchants, farmers and teamsters, Yvonne was born. She learned early in life—who told her?—that her birth was a mistake. Her father, Guillerme, bought pills that were meant to induce an abortion, but her mother, Irene, flushed them down the toilet. So, on that July day, the midwife was summoned to the two-family house in a quiet corner of town to help deliver into this hostile world a tiny, squalling, freckled, red-headed girl. And Guillerme couldn't prevent it.

He did the next best thing. While Irene was in the throes of labor, Guillerme did his own squalling: railing against his young wife, accusing her of having the baby by another man. As a result, Yvonne's earliest world outside the womb was a tumble of life and death, an ambiguous amalgam of acceptance and rejection. With such a start, how could she ever know that she was ever accepted?

She would recall the tentative nature of her family life, the frequent moves: to New York City, to the bread lines of New Bedford, to Lisbon, Portugal where her father was born and where he died eighty-six years later, back to the States finally to settle in a cold-water tenement apartment in Hoboken. Except for a younger sister, her childhood there was one of loneliness and melancholy.

As a young, impressionable and sensitive child she bore the burden of entering this world unwanted by her father (though he, in later years, gave her the affection she needed), and understandably, resented by her mother. It seems as though she carried with her, like some genetic marker on her psychic double helix, the inner code that whispered over and over: "Life isn't for you; you're in the way, expendable, the cause of trouble." Could she have finally said no to so contradictory a birth and life?

Often a sickly child, she was also high-strung, nervous, given to emotional crises. She suffered what doctors called a nervous breakdown while in high school, another upon graduating from college, and a spell of post-partum depression after our first child. Then for the next twenty years, except for fleeting episodes of emotional hurt, she handled life resourcefully, creatively, and happily. During her last three years, again she grew seriously depressed and agitated, frequently anxious, and for a time she sought relief in alcohol. After a couple of years in psychotherapy she began to show progress and it looked as though we would soon see bright light at the end of the tunnel. With that kind of confidence, we spent our thirtieth wedding anniversary in Bermuda, our only trip out of the country. That single vacation was to be our last.

Then she made her final move. I am inclined to see it, when considering all of the aforementioned conditions of her life, as a sacrificial gift to the family she loved, to the community that loved her. She made that most painful decision possible, one that can never be called back. She made her final protest to what must have been an unbearable world; she put an end to the torment; and somehow, on her own, cast out the demons that haunted her fragile soul.

On a recent trip to the Netherlands with my daughter, we visited the RijksMuseum Van Gogh in Amsterdam and the Kroller-Muller Museum near Appledoorn to saturate ourselves with the fabulous collection of Van Gogh's paintings displayed there. It was like a religious experience to stand so close to genius, to observe the sensitive capturing of light, the brilliant colors, the depths of feeling as evident in the master's mad and marvelous works. Although not among these collections, his familiar "Starry Night" suggests to me more than any other the painter's wrenching struggle with beauty and suffering, with life and death.

I keep watching for the faintest twinkling stars to erupt into meteors that light up the heavens and the earth. I keep listening for whatever songs the spheres of nature and angels have to sing. The voices and images of sorrow continue to fade into that dim past and there is left for me enough of a glimmer of hope that turns night into day, enough color to splash with beauty the world that is left for me.

This world of wonder is not the one in which we make our living. It is the stuff of fantasy, fiction, overblown myth. So we have Wonder Woman and Wonder Boy, even Wonder Bread. We know none of it is real, but a part of us keeps hoping nonetheless.

We are told in this scientific age that there are no spontaneous actions, no *a priori* realities, no luck—good or bad, no mystery, no real Wonder Woman. A cause and effect exists for everything and nothing happens that can't be explained. We live in a time that makes the scientific inquiry of Newton's look like alchemy.

My wife and I grew up with the scientific method: make your observations, gather and organize your data, formulate your hypotheses, run them through again and again, and then draw your conclusions. So I submit the agonizing shock of her death to continuing scrutiny, at any moment of the day, in the middle of the night. It has stuck itself in the grooves of my mind. Yet I know and understand no more now than at the beginning. Her death, like all deaths, is final. It can't be run through the distillation tubes, weighed on the balance, or plotted on a graph. The computers spit it out. Neither the software nor the laboratory procedure has been designed to handle the big question of death.

Our neatly constructed universe can be so boringly predictable. Scientists can prophesy the existence of sub-atomic particles before they are discovered. They predict new stars, energy fields, and other stuff in far-out space before they produce the equipment to locate them. Gaps in the fossil record make the study of life forms a bit less sure, and it is life itself that happily fills the Earth with endless variety and novelty. Our own histories befuddle the prognosticators even more.

Human life, with its emotion, creativity, intellect, goes beyond simple variety; it fills the planet with all kinds of surprises! What ought to happen doesn't, and what shouldn't does. Even if our environment were fixed and ordered, our behavior remains ambiguous and confused.

My confusion makes up a big chunk of my grief. It is a confusion that keeps asking through the tears: "Why?" "Where does this fit into the grander scheme of things?" "What, if anything, does it all mean?" In this present moment I can't tolerate life without certainty, experience without knowable cause, questions without available answers. It's so confusing.

We walk by faith and not sight.

Agreed. It is axiomatic to our religion. But not to our behavior. My grief demands some empirical demonstration so that from now on I can also walk by sight. I don't like stumbling blindfold out of this dark chasm. I want the roadmaps to be up-to-date and accurate. I wish to trace every red or blue line straight to my destiny. I need to know the names of each crossroad that marks my progress, each little town, county seat.

Here I am, though, sightless in Gaza, but without the strength of a Samson to pull down the temples of all my idol gods. I worship too much at the clay feet of reason, cause and effect, science. I insist on asking questions, knowing why; and I can't seem to get on with life until I do know. Or until I let the questions, along with their answers, lie still in the rubble of my broken world.

Can religion come to my aid? I should have the answers; after all, I am a man of God whose faith should be unshakable. I've studied theology, and theology—the "queen of the sciences"—tells all.

No, theology doesn't tell all. There are as many gaps in theology as there are in science's search for a unified force theory. Science isn't content with Einstein's amazing discoveries of relativity, nor was he. Instead, it seeks diligently to find a single answer to every what, why, and how of nature. Likewise, theology betrays its impatience by going beyond its subject and seeks clearer, more precise information and know-how. Our theologies often crave the security of knowing all rather than running the risk of knowing only God.

Theologizing often misses the mark in its approach to grief and death; and theologians are growing increasingly aware of this shortcoming. In the days of her death dozens of clergymen—some astute theologians—came to be at my side. Not one of them tried to provide the answer or end to the story. Unlike Job's sidekicks arguing for the logic of retribution, my friends were virtually mute in the face of my affliction. And by being so, they went away carrying a share of the burden.

Faith for me is now the courage to get on with life without all the answers. Grace is the strength that makes all possible.

It is grace that opens our hearts to a world of mystery and wonder that accepts the unknowable, the uncertain, the unanswered—that makes life what it is.

Who wants a world without mystery and intrigue, without the wonderful and amazing? Who really seeks a world without dangers and risks, always predictable and secure? It would certainly be a dull place, a world where freedom could never be exercised. In that light, I can only accept my wife's untimely death as evidence of freedom. This world into which God calls us to make do is fraught with a great variety of freedom's possibilities, as improbable as they appear.

"No pain, no gain." You can hear the phrase in the world of physical exercise and conditioning. Muscles that feel no pain are probably getting neither stronger nor more flexible. It presents an analogy for the exercise of the heart. Those who run the risk of genuine love alone must worry about emotional pain. The more friends; the more good-byes—and the more wakes to attend, the more graves to visit, the more deaths to share. Those who truly live life to the fullest will bear the full cup of suffering. Only those who are willing to pay the price in pain and anguish find life full to the brim. Happy people also suffer; they are no more lucky than the rest. They create their own happiness. That's the rule of thumb.

Some thumbs, however, don't seem to rule very well. Slogans and catch-words, for all their conventional wisdom, fail to carry the whole weight of truth; they leave too much room for false inferences. "No pain, no gain" may leave one with nothing but pain—an intolerable amount of it. There is simply no guarantee that pain will bring gain, that hardship will yield happiness, that suffering will make one a better person. It may; but it's not inevitable.

Some suffering just ends there, and I wonder if *this* was not the hollow suffering and useless pain that she knew? What awful single event switched her off from life and on to death? I keep asking that, but my grief keeps bringing me back to the unanswered and unanswerable. It won't let me go.

Because so much remains unclear I find myself collecting doubts as though they were trading stamps. So far I have nowhere to cash them in. I have a fist full of doubts about the quality of life I gave her, about the kind of love and affection I offered her, about the misgivings and hurts I put in her mind and how they may have piled up to an unbearable level. Was life with me so bad? To admit I have faults takes no courage or exceptional honesty. She could easily detect mine every day. It is those faults of which I have been unaware, or deliberately avoided, that are beginning to madden me. I wish now she might have been less kind and told me at point-blank range when I was wrong-headed, impossible, stubborn, thoughtless. But pride often gets in the way of the truth.

Though I don't want to believe I was the cause of her despair, I find it equally difficult to affirm myself as a decent husband. Like a cautious gambler I hedge all my bets, in one hand holding on to each doubt, on the other, rationalizing her death as though it were the logical choice and discarding every misgiving. But neither doubt nor certainty assuage death and grief. Either way, it's a bad deal.

Although the question "Why?" is neither answerable nor understandable, it spills out of my anguish. It is at once useless to ponder and yet the most generative of all exercises in this time of sorrow. It may not provide the answer, but it will carry a long way in dealing with the pain and loss. From "Why?" our minds start asking "What?" "How?" "Where to?"

For example, when my wife died I was in the midst of an active search for a change in parishes. I didn't need to run away; my congregation and I have been through thick and thin together for sixteen years. Our relationship is strong and healthy, but we tend to grow stale and too comfortable next to each other. I am fully aware of the trends that accompany a twenty-year pastorate: nothing happens, and no one seems to care. I don't want that for me or the church I serve. So I am faced with the question: How will her death and my widowhood affect my vocation? Could I make a move at this emotion-laden point in my life? Dare I plunge into so many new relationships, an entirely new setting and ministry without a half of me being present? Do I have the capacity to work through a year of grief without the aid and support of those friends I know so well, those people who loved both her and me? Would it be fair to disrupt further the life of a congregation that has already been jolted by the tragic death of their pastor's wife? And if the answers to all of the above are no, then what do I do?

Questions of property rise up more frequently. The state reminds me coldly that I own half of what's rightfully mine since my spouse died intestate. It refers to her "estate" as though she were a wealthy dowager. The problems will work out in time: as much as the bureaucracy needs.

Seven years ago we purchased a small vacation home not far from where I presently live. We had no problem meeting the payments so long as she was employed, and she would gladly work for that little home to call her own. She kept our tiny cabin in the woods looking like a fairy cottage nestled in a parkland. No weeds, no leaves lying around, everything was kept green, orderly, as neat as a pin. I am not sure I can do either: keep the place neat or make all those payments. But neither do I want to give it up. Her death strikes me like a dirty divorce: breaking up what has become dear and precious—for economic reasons alone. Economics now take precedence to the coinage of the heart, and I doubt that contributes to my wise handling of this grief.

If my assets are vulnerable, my ego is even more so. Again and again there charges into the foreground of my thoughts a subject that usually remains silent. In one short moment I was reduced from a sexually active male to a eunuch. I never chose celibacy as a lifestyle; I am still a Protestant! But in one twist of fate it was thrust upon me; death is an episode that castrates as cleanly as a surgeon's scalpel.

As the days of grief take their toll, those strong feelings become gradually sublimated; there are just too many details of life to tend to. The awful surprise came, however, in the early days after her death. I would wake in the middle of the night and reach out for her, and she was not there! With that empty reaching came the realization that she never will be there for me again, snuggling up to warm herself and relax her body for sleep, or to arouse and awaken mine.

We take for granted such gifts of normal day-to-day life. Now gone, the human side of our lives can't automatically be shut off from them. The shock of the grief, the overtime work of the brain, the emotional exhaustion surely shut off those urgings. But for how long? I was particularly surprised by this sense of loss, and how vulnerable it made me feel, and how ugly I felt after that. My lover and beloved, my poor pained bride of thirty years was gone, and the age-old ache of Eros was tugging at me. Again, the Protestant in me knows guilt when he sees it and nudges pleasure aside when he feels it.

It isn't the sexual act that obsesses the grieving; it is one's personhood bound up in being man or woman that is so violated by the death of the spouse that the entire ego is shattered. Death reduces me to a neuter, an object. I am no longer the subject in the wonderful drama of human affection.

This, of course, raises another looming question: How do I conduct myself as an "it" in the months or years to come? How do I guard my fragile male ego against the attempted seductions that up to now I have never noticed? Will I be strong enough to resist some silly and shallow romantic entanglement for which one day I would be sorry? I still need love and affection; it is foolishness I must do without.

Sympathy deals with death, but only with death. We are left pretty much alone to deal with the issues that death drags in by the heels. In grief life takes the shape of a giant question mark, and it tightens its closing spiral around us, squeezing from us all the breath of our certainties. We struggle with the unanswered and the unanswerable. Whether we've ever had a formal religion or not, now we must walk by faith.

6

The Dark Embrace

Death is at work in us.
St. Paul

And that's the way it is.
Walter Cronkite

The rains keep falling, making these short, dark days of December even more dreary. I awaken in the morning to my own inner clock—much later than my accustomed hour. I have no idea what time it is or what time means. It's simply a hand sweeping a circle, a trigger that flicks off one liquid crystal digit and shines another in its place. I have no sense of timing and don't really care what calendars or clocks announce. I make few appointments, and need to keep almost none. The time keepers of my normal days and months no longer operate.

After more than two weeks I have yet to listen to one word from a radio. I watched two science programs on public television, no more. The newspaper arrives at the doorstep each day, but I give it only a cursory glance. Once an inveterate weather watcher, I don't care whether it rains or shines, freezes or thaws. I haven't the slightest idea where the Dow Jones stands or what goes on in the political arena. The world apparently keeps turning, a man goes on surviving with his artificial heart, and our government presumably pulses in its own arena as well.

The crush at the post office tells me we're moving toward Christmas, as do the abundance of colored lights strung around rows of houses and trees. The traffic on the roads near our home, which is within two miles of six major shopping centers, grinds to a turtle's pace. I can guess what occupies the minds of those milling mobs joining the cash register queues.

But the Christmas wreath that hangs silently on my front door refuses to conceal that single transparent fact: someone has died, and I am dying, too.

Tomorrow I shall be back to God's house to hear the word of the Lord. I had brashly, albeit honestly, expected by now to have returned to the pulpit. After all, I am strong, I can weather the storms whether they are thrown my way by December, sickness, oppression, grief, whatever. However, after only two weeks, my soul is still numb, my mind draws only a blank, my body feels like rubber. My wounds are still gaping; it will take a long time for them to heal over.

Nevertheless, before she died I had already planned the sermon for the Third Sunday in Advent with its sentimental-

64

ly clever title: "It's Beginning to Smell Like Christmas." Now, it doesn't merely smell. It stinks.

It reeks partly because I shall miss so much of it. My dear wife loved Christmas trees so much that there were times she would continue to decorate ours after December 25th! She shopped tirelessly. On Christmas morning she would once again become the innocent child, opening the smallest trifle as though it were a king's ransom, lavishing gratitude for every gift, waiting expectantly for the rest of us to do the same. Now she's gone and the brightness of that day has dimmed. I have no desire to hang garlands or set up candles or turn on the lights. Darkness covers me.

From this down-to-earth perspective, where none of the tinsel trimmings of Yuletide touch my fancy, I smell the decay of a celebration down the road. The music tells the story: "Grandma got run over by a reindeer," "Jingle Bells" (sung by dogs!), "All I want for Christmas is my upper plate," beside 150 million recordings of "White Christmas."

I read in *Harper's*, December 1984: FAO Schwarz expects to sell 10,000 robots this Christmas season; the 400 richest Americans have a combined net of 125 billion dollars; in the event of a nuclear freeze, an estimated 250,000 jobs would be lost; 24% of our American teachers wouldn't teach if they could start over.

Neiman Marcus comes up again with its cute $20,000 gift suggestion. VCRs and personal computers will be the big retail sellers for old Santa. Dewars paints a holiday landscape with its white labels. A bedraggled Santa Claus slumps on a

bar stool next to Duffy in the cartoon strip: "Call me Nick."
A middle-aged, dumpy-shaped man sings along, "He rules
the earth," while idling a ton of pollutants from his gas-guz-
zling car. The sorrow of frankincense and the pain of myrrh
are lost in the largess of fool's gold.

The wreath hangs on my front door and nobody seems to
understand; it speaks as much of a funeral as a Christmas
decoration. A life has slipped out of this house; the halls are
suddenly hushed; an unholy silence falls upon these once
vibrant rooms whose doors are forever sealed against her
return. Only the greens hint at some small measure of hope,
eternity, and life for us.

That is what Christmas and Advent are all about. They lay
bare every human endeavor to cover up our death with glitter
and our dying with styrofoam snow. The bells of the season
announce one indisputable fact: this age of ours is in the
throes of death and its only hope is in the coming of the Son
of Man. His coming is disguised in that paradox of death and
the cross, the life-and-death struggle of a stable birth, the
arrogance of a Herod's tyranny, the demonic striving to pull
down the stars from their heavens, an empty tomb. "You will
call his name Jesus, for he will save his people from their
sins."

Christmas, unlike that shallow, mindless hoax we have
made of it, is the cosmic reminder that "we are being killed
all the day long."

Grief is the embrace of death. We can't escape it. Once
someone you truly love dies, your own dying accelerates.

More than any other human experience or emotion, grief puts us in touch with our own mortality.

We must clarify that, however. Healthy grief—and there is such a kind of suffering—doesn't allow the sorrowing to be obsessed with death, or suggest that he may collapse from a massive coronary attack on the very next day. It doesn't accompany him from a funeral parlor and urge him to look both ways before crossing the street. When reading of a neighbor's death notice in the morning paper, one in healthy grief doesn't explore his own body for malignant growths. There is a vast difference between grief and neurosis.

Nor is grief the painfully revealing light that comes through the window of mid-life crisis. Those who have been pulled through such a wringer of torment will recognize the agonizing introspection and self-loathing, the dead weight of despair and hopelessness as a kind of burial, a heavy dose of genuine grief, a dying of a part of one's self that makes room for the growth and acceptance of another. At certain stages in life's journey we do come in contact with mortality, especially when all the myths of our immortality are at least cognitively put to rest. Grownups, as well as guileless children, accept the premise that all of us one day will pass from this scene.

We know this by virtue of our thinking; the recognition is on an intellectual level. When Yvonne died, however, I truly felt death at work within me. A significant part of me was gone, never to return. Death still stabs at me repeatedly, and from its assaults there is no relief.

So, in a sense, I celebrate Christmas as never before, appropriately, sincerely, sorrowfully. The radio and television are blank and silent. My own bad news is repeated again and again in its own strained, staccato voice: "She is gone. A part of you has died."

I don't subscribe to that old notion that the longer we live with another person the more alike we grow. Perhaps that happens enough to convince people that it is possible. But such was certainly not our case. She was the one with light in her eyes, a buoyancy in her step, abundant energy in every act. I, on the other hand, tended to plod along, my face a blank piece of paper. Our life together was often a tenuous balancing act, a tug-of-war between opposites, a tension of such disparate qualities.

I was the romantic with my head in the sky, my feet in the nineteenth century, my loyalties to the likes of Theodore Roosevelt. She, a pragmatist of the twentieth century, had her feet on the ground, her roots planted in the no-nonsense politics of Franklin Roosevelt. We shared a broad spectrum of musical tastes but I would fantasize to the rich stuff of Tchaikovsky, Liszt, Smetana; she enjoyed Mussorgski, Copland, Hohvannes.

I was the suburban Dutch Calvinist who read Hemingway, Steinbeck, DeVries, E.B. White, the Old Testament. She was from the inner city, a Roman Catholic who read Michener, Oates, Millay, Chandler, Azimov, and Paul's letter to the Romans. I liked food laced with sugar; she doused hers in oil and vinegar. I could eat ice cream by the quart; she would smother otherwise perfectly good food with horseradish. I wanted my apple pie cold; hers had to be hot. She needed three blankets and slept on her back like a queen. I got by with one blanket and curled on my side like a serf.

We balanced all of these variations on a single theme throughout our life together, one giving in at times a little more than the other. The extremes of our two temperaments and personalities more often than not blended together, not so much like the pigments of the artist's palette or the nuances of fine wine, but as a tossed salad or a camper's stew.

Over those thirty years all of her attributes, varied as they were from mine, became a part of me. We granted to each other individuality yet found energy in our oneness. She wouldn't have me near her grocery cart and stayed a mile away from my sloppy desk. Yet in the larger matters of the heart, we were one. When she died something in me—something fundamentally me—died too. And I can't get it back or revive it. I can only wait and hope for resurrection, for rebirth, for the long-expected day with Simeon. Someday I shall surrender all my hopes and dreams, letting go of them in peace, having been content with the salvation of the Lord.

7

Guilt

He shall purify the sons of Levi.
Isaiah

Whatever became of sin?
Karl Menninger

The snow was blowing hard and covering the roads with a slick teflon coating as I pulled into the filling station. The gas jockey emerged from his cocoon of warmth and topped off my tank. "I hope it keeps snowing," he said. "I don't want it to rain." Most of our snow storms on the eastern seaboard usually do change to rain, but on this December day we were in for quite a pile of white stuff before the rains took over.

Along with the young gas station attendant, a lot of folks who remain up north like the snow. I don't know why. It tends to get terribly messy, falls down your collar and into your boots, makes travel complicated, and around the city looks ugly in one short day.

But in those first few hours there is a freshness to it, a serenity, a quiet beauty. It was during those earliest hours of our first snowfall of the year I drove over to the cemetery, to her new grave. The evergreen blankets were all but invisible, yesterday's flowers were buried, individual plots were blurred into a single common grave. Trees stretched black fingers skyward, as if in benediction. Everything was still, silent, hushed. The falling crystals soaked up every decibel of noise, cushioned every footstep, muffled every voice. I stopped my car in the faint tire traces of the one vehicle that had preceded mine, killed the engine, turned off the wiper, the defroster, the radio. I rolled down the widow to listen for the silence, to be touched and stung by the icy burning of the purifying crystals that were blowing over and blanketing her bed. "I love you," I whispered. "I'm so sorry; I'm so sad." And once again: "Why? My dear, oh why?" Tears warmed my cold face as I drove away.

I didn't notice the snow for the rest of the day. I would be glad for the sun to shine and melt it all away. Yet, for that single moment, there was a sense of cleansing, purity, good.

Although people love snow and talk about it around Christmas, you hear few of them speak of purity. There is one piece of music, however, that often creeps in at this time of year and sings that theme. During our advent of grief my daughters pulled our an old scratchy album of Handel's "Messiah" and played its familiar strains. I must give credit where credit is due: Mr. Handel surely had a winner there. There may be better sacred music but surely none so widely loved, none that has touched so many lives. I listen to it every year, never tire of it, and hope to hear it performed sometime in a place like Carnegie Hall or the Cathedral of St. John the Divine. For now, our little record player will have to do.

I seem to know most of it by heart, I've heard it so often. Yet I never truly hear it all. Some of the choruses and recitatives get lost in the air as I wait for the "good" parts. This year I really heard for the first time "He shall purify the sons of Levi" and felt that the Mormon Tabernacle Choir, way off in Salt Lake City over a decade ago, was singing about me.

As I pine away nights that are insufferably long and try to make some sense of my tangled days, as I break down on the shoulder of a caring family member, as I sob openly at the Christmas Eve service, I hear burning in my ears, "He shall purify—the sons of Levi." And I finally grasp what it is all about.

At least I think I do. I have for that text a feeling I've never before had. I see myself in the lineage of the sons of Levi, a temple handyman, a religious professional whose stylus is stuck in the groove, repeating the right spiritual laws at the right time, an ecclesiastical mechanic who tries his level best to keep the pious machinery running as smoothly as a Swiss watch (of course, it never does). I am of that ancient fraternity which carries prayers around on phylacteries or in the breast pocket of my Sears serge suit, who hands out soporific slogans like so many sleeping pills to the spiritually restless, and like a hanging judge, hands down judgment on the sinners. But the priests who prescribe their purgatories to the poor souls must first pass through the fires and scramble out from their own ash heaps.

He shall purify the sons of Levi.

He shall baptize you with the Holy Spirit and with fire.

Though your sins be as scarlet, they shall be as white as snow.

The snows are falling white today out of the burning red furnace of my anguish. God refines his gold and the dross settles around me like frozen cinders spewed out from the smoke stack of my grief. I feel the fire; I feel the ice.

No law says it must be that way. Ministers of the Word can still preach that Word in sincerity whether or not they pass through the fires. They can be good pastors without having suffered in person everything their parishioners have. One of the clergy can teach some truth and wisdom that hasn't yet been burned into his own life just as a celibate priest can provide marriage counseling.

Surely we don't need to maneuver our marriages to the rocks so that we can better understand the divorces that are tearing apart the families around us. We don't offer our children to Molech so we can minister effectively to the young couple whose four year old was mangled by a truck. We don't rob banks to get in touch with jailbirds or burn our Bibles so we can converse with the village atheist.

All I know is that this one son of Levi is going through the fire, and whether he is going to be a better pastor for it remains questionable, and, furthermore, irrelevant; whether he comes out of the ordeal as pure as gold and white as snow remains highly doubtful. It is simply his fire. It is his flame searing his heart; they are his hot coals that shape something about him in his forge; it is his white heat that cauterizes the stinking flesh of his unique life.

And the snow that falls today is also his, covering the tracks of all his journeys and his wanderings. No one can ever know where he's been. His travels are now obliterated, the paths are all lost to the blinding whiteness, his yesterdays disappear under a million silver crystals. He cannot retrace his steps to any other moment of time in his life. They are gone; he is alone to start anew.

I have seen grief mingled with guilt before and wondered how nasty people could be so sorrowful when their time for weeping came. Perhaps this is the part of grief that bites the most. As St. Paul asserts in his treatise on life and death in 1 Corinthians 15: "The sting of death is sin." I could never quite fathom the word order as it is rendered in the English Bible. My rational mind automatically reversed it to make another sense: the sting of sin is death. That corresponds with the other texts the Apostle is remembered for and it fits nicely into my way of looking at things. You sin; you die. Period. Death is the fallout of the cosmic disaster; the creature has rebelled against the creator and gets his due. But try as I may, I am still faced with this strange sequence of Paul's text. "The sting of death is sin." And my sorrow from her death leaves me covered with welts as though I had plunged into a hornet's nest. I've been stung, again and again, and the fire creeps under my skin. I cry out for relief and there is none. I'd jump into a cold lake or roll in that blowing snow to ease the pain. The pain, however, doesn't go away. Death continues to sting, and the sting has the feel of sin.

I am not wallowing in guilt. Friends won't allow that. "Don't blame yourself for what has happened. You did all you could," they say. I'd like to agree that I did all that was humanly possible; at the same time I disagree. No one, with few exceptions, does all he can. Perhaps Michelangelo did; or Mozart, Shakespeare, even Einstein. Most of us fall short of our potential and we need not possess genius to do more. No one can convince me that I've done all I could; and I must live with that sting. I continue to wonder what more I might have done that awful day, or what I could have said that week. What possibly could I have done or been throughout our lifetime together to make her feel differently about herself and life? Somehow life cheated her—that's how she saw it—and I was a big part of her life.

Not that I cheated on her; at least I had not in those most obvious ways. No other woman came into my life in those thirty years; I was either too ugly, naive, or good; and I'd prefer to discuss none of the possibilities. Probably none of those have any bearing on the situation. That I might have cheated would now make me feel foul; that I hadn't, nonetheless, makes me feel no better. There are myriad ways I could have done her in: robbed her of security, of self-worth, self-esteem, tender love when she needed it, not when I felt like offering it. No one can tell me I did all I could for her.

Too many times I found my heart wander from her. The raindrops of our personal storms so easily magnified our personal differences, and anger often wedged itself between us. Rather than rainbows we cast menacing shadows where our paths crossed and blanked out the joy that should have been there. At times she could become deeply unhappy, and I would find myself wondering what life might be like with a spontaneously joyful woman. I grew impatient and testy and sick of her being sick; and now I feel sick from that.

In death we are touched and stung by sin. There is no way to get out from under its burden. The *mea culpa* follows.

Wherever it originates, the guilt I feel is subtle. Perhaps in some psychic niche there is a part of my being that is especially hard on itself, or there is some universal measure of guilt in all of us. It draws me back to an unanswerable and even irrelevant question: "Why couldn't it have been me?" I face and feel the guilt of survivorship. She's gone and I am left. She's among the dead, and I am among the living; and there's something intrinsically, shamefully wrong with that. Even though it may not be directly my fault, it should not be like this. I feel the guilt because there is no way I can remove myself from the picture. A line, a pigment, a shadow, some light nuance of composition—I'm there. That she, in the prime of life, should be removed from *us* is a photograph out of focus, over-exposed, a painting smeared and marred before it could be framed.

My surviving her exacerbates this grief. No matter whether it is appropriate or not, this is the way it is. All the platitudes and offerings in the world can make this burden of mine no lighter.

Another kind of foolish guilt raises its head. For want of a better description, I call it my guilt for not being God. Her death leaves me feeling helpless just when I feel I should be invincible. I'm human, weak and powerless; and I don't like it. I want to be divine, have all the answers, shout the commands, captain the ship we call the universe and get her back on course, back to the safety of some cosmic harbor. I would bring my darling back, give her another chance, breathe life into her empty frame, be rid of this whole damned mess that has mucked up my life so badly.

Somehow we must listen to the voice of our guilt. It is often the one voice we can fully trust. We live in a society that shuns guilt, hardly knows it. It is drummed into us: "Don't feel guilty." No one wants to pay the price of reconciliation, of atonement, of forgiveness. Never feeling guilt means never being in touch with what is true about the human condition.

So let me feel for awhile the sting of sin and guilt. I know no way to yank it from my grief without tearing the whole cloth. I wait with Simeon for the consolation of Israel. I stand alone in the cleft of the rock with complaining Elijah. I need to feel the fires that purify the sons of Levi. And it is those fires that melt the ice that glistens on the edges of my heart.

8

Anger

Be angry, but sin not.
St. Paul

Do not go gentle into that good night,
Rage, rage, against the dying of the light.
Dylan Thomas

"Oh God. She's gone. No! No!" As I remember them, these were the opening words of my grief's monologue. Our deepest pains are sure to be directed toward God even as our dashed dreams leave us wondering why and where he's gone. The sudden realization that she had left me in such a final, irrevocable way struck me in a spatial dimension: she is not here, she's gone away. I keep crying the "No!"—not so much a denial because the living survivor has no such luxury as denial—but as a protest.

Death is and must be met with protest. It is far too great an outrage to be accepted without a murmur of complaint. And

79

any protest that fits the magnitude of the event demands the energy of anger and rage.

For a month I wondered where in my grief and torn-up heart I would find some natural anger. I knew that accepting anger was a part of healthy grief, and expecting it to erupt, I found myself struggling to get in touch with it. It just wasn't there.

Perhaps we can take only so much feeling at once. I reached a saturation point with shock, sorrow, longing, suffering all bursting upon me with unbearable fierceness. Is it possible that I would find relief faster if I would simply shake my clenched fist at God and challenge him to make sense for me of this awful puzzle? I couldn't afford to get mad yet; just bearing the hurt was about all I could manage for the present.

My anger surfaced about a month after she died, while I was making every effort to get back into the routine of daily life. (Routine is such a misnomer; I'll never find myself living the same life I have heretofore known so familiarly.) I rose a little earlier on that last day of the year, lingered over my first cup of tea, and began the physical workout that had become a part of my daily life. Exercise is good for me, the doctors say. So whether I'm in the mood, happy or miserable, I begin the day with some form of exercise, work up a sweat, take an invigorating warm shower, feed the body.

I had always done my calisthenics alone, my long walks alone, my bike rides alone—except for those days my faithful dog trotted at my side. The first cup of tea or coffee was usually alone too. She often lovingly brought it to me, but we rarely sat down to have breakfast or that eye-opening cup together. So carrying out my morning activities shouldn't have seemed very different. The difference, nonetheless, was real.

When my wife was around, life and action surrounded me. She skipped past my grunting hulk as I was doing my morning sit-ups; she made small talk as she ran in and out of the different rooms, and that made the day brighter; her dashing around the kitchen added a measure of life to my breakfast. Now it is morbidly quiet and still.

I was sweating away, that last day of the year, at my daily dozen, stretching, bending, lifting dumbbells. A morning news show on the TV broke the silence and drew attention away from myself. The network featured Peter Duchin playing old songs on the piano, a sentimental send-off for another year. The sweet strains of "Someone to Watch Over Me" touched me with a mixed bag of emotions.

It reminded me of her singing. She knew so many of the old show tunes and as she worked her coloratura soprano would fill the house. Those were happy moments; when she sang, no one could be unhappy. But the piano playing that last day of the year also angered me. Like a jealous, selfish child, I felt neglected. There *was* no one to watch over me.

I gazed beyond my breakfast to a stove and counter top that were too neat to be real. Her books and lunch bags were missing from the table. The messy coffee cups she often left behind in haste were also absent. The room was filled with emptiness and quiet. I was alone; only lingering thoughts accompanied me. I thought of little things she enjoyed doing: in the fall, to rake leaves and ready the yard for winter's bleak visit; in the spring, to prune and manicure every bush and shrub. We accumulated tools and gadgets to make her gardening easier and more fun. There are neither tools nor gadgets to make the tending of my lonely life any fun. It is not the routine but the repetition: exercise, breakfast, thoughts—all alone.

"Damn it!" I shouted, pounding my fist on table and wall. "No. No! You should not have done that! Why, why did you do it?" I repeated again and again. Now something inside me was angry with her, and it was exploding all over the place. I must protest her death and therefore her decision to die and leave me this way.

Somehow we come to the junction along the road of emotions where we must choose to take either the path of rage or despair. I'm afraid my wife could never express her anger adequately, even when there was an accumulation of it exploding within her fragile soul. She turned those feelings inward, she manifested hurt rather than rage; she became desperate rather than determined. I came to a point in my own grief where my only options were to pine away in despair or explode in anger. It was no deliberate choice; it just happened.

This rage is really not directed toward her. It is pointed toward an "it," an undefinable, intangible, all-encompassing frustration and futility that fills my time and overwhelms my thoughts. I can't get myself to direct anger toward her; I must not.

"Be angry, but sin not." There must, therefore, be something positive about this rage of mine. I struggle to find a position between fight or flee. A great deal of me tries to flee, to run away, to escape what is real. If I could run far enough, I could get away from every vestige of pain, the memories, the shock, the despair. But none of us can travel that far. Wherever we go we're bound to carry with us the baggage of our hurts and disappointments. Wherever we retreat we will face enemies that are even more threatening.

Grief knows an anger that stands on middle ground, neither wallowing in a quagmire of defeat nor running pell-mell to attack every irritation. This anger is the protest that shouts at the top of its lungs: "No! No, I'm tired of being hurt, so stop! I won't stand for this any longer!" "Even you, death, must stop what you are doing to me. I can't and won't accept it!"

So I pound the table and slam the door. I join the thousands of this race who must give vent to the steam of their passion in every direction and in no particular direction. We protest because death is a rotten, filthy enemy that fights unfairly and puts us at a disadvantage. And the continuing disadvantage creates in us an ugly, cantankerous disposition.

In my protest, in my anger, I think about the wrath of God. We Bible readers are a bit uncomfortable with that language and relegate it to the remoteness of the Old Testament. There, we foolishly assert, we read of the righteous God while in the

New Testament we hear of our loving God. But who are we to divide God into parts? Who dares malign his righteousness and strip it of mercy? And who would eviscerate his mercy and empty it of justice? God is God, kind and angry at once, the God of Abraham, Isaac, and Jacob, and the Father of our Lord Jesus Christ. His wrath is that anger that rises out of his hurt, the rage appropriate to his disappointment, the ire that must attend the pain and agony of the cross. The wrath of God is God's *No!* It is his protest, whether loud or quiet, against the gathering shadows, against the raging storm, against the fading of the light and the dying of life.

It would be presumptuous for me to equate my anger with God's, but I feel they are made of basically the same stuff. That doesn't make my indignation righteous. It simply gets me in touch with the quality of anger that accompanies my grief.

This anger of grief compares to the grieving of Jesus who was touched by the suffering all around him. It is the anger that threw the money-changers out of the Temple, that called dogs, dogs, and snakes, snakes, that names the demons and casts them back to hell where they belong.

We mortals play with fire when we take into our own hands the kind of anger Jesus expressed. We are equally in danger of being scorched if we sit idly by and allow the demons to run amok. We must say *No!*, raise our voices to the heavens, stomp our feet until we shake hell. *It must not be!*

Grief stands at the interface of life and death. On the side of life, I want to wage war with my opponent, Death. That is at the core of my feeling.

"I hate them with a perfect hatred," said the Psalmist. Those words rise like an ugly face from a beautiful song. But what is a perfect hatred when our understanding leaves no room at all for any kind of hatred? Do I, in my sorrow, stoop so low as to fly into a tantrum, rail at my neighbor, and thus dishonor the name of God? The Psalmist was aiming his arrows at those who hated God, whoever they were. Any behavior, any action, any rebellion that flies in the face of God must not be tolerated. Goodness must not remain silent in the face of injustice and evil. The demonic must be dealt with, named for what it is, wrestled to the ground, cast out. This is what I believe the Psalmist meant. It likewise reflects the anger that wells up in me.

We cannot, however, give in to the danger of allowing our personal complaints and enemies to take on the shape of ogres. We mustn't permit them to metamorphose into the ugly trolls that frighten us off the bridge and hinder our progress. There are much bigger devils running loose to deal with. Grief is deeply personal, and we cannot escape its devastating effect on our lives. It is in our grief we overturn every stone and uncover every little troublesome pest. And we uncover every tiny cherished object.

The objects of my anger do not belong to everyone else; they aren't universal enemies. But they resemble those of everyone else. They are shared in common not so much for what they are but for how they are perceived. My enemies and foes, my ogres and trolls, though not contributing directly, nonetheless have exacerbated her death and my pain.

My wife spent over twelve years of her last years in a single school system as a tenured and beloved teacher. But school systems, as I see them in our area, are no longer interested in quality teaching as a first priority. Their concern is first of all a whittled-down bare-bones budget, bones to throw to myopic taxpayers. Nothing in the system rewards good teachers or good teaching; plenty in the system rewards the incompetent and protects those who just hang on. During those years, some of the best classroom teachers, along with my wife, were being dismissed regularly; administrators, at the same time, were given higher wages. The teachers' unions suck the dues out of conscientious public servants only to proffer shelter to the lazy.

When this calling to which she was devoted collapsed around her, she began to die. I could see it happen; the anxiety, the depression. Her once joyful vocation became a drudgery, her commitment grew indifferent, her boundless energies and excitement began gradually to wane. And no one seemed to care; they hid behind the rules, they covered their own flanks. And I hate them with a "perfect hatred."

I am angry with the medical establishment, too. What it could do in her case remains doubtful. She worried about early signs of Alzheimer's Disease, but so little is known about the disease that medical help would have benefitted her little. We accept that limited knowledge as though it were totally appropriate. But we should not. I bristle with anger every time I must bury a young victim of cancer, knowing that millions are spent on research and very little gain in the cure rate can be demonstrated. I grow impatient with the foot-dragging and the self-righteous attitude of those in the medical profession who reap riches from the misery of the sick and suffering. Fortunes are spent on the latest diagnostic tools, CAT and PET scanners, sophisticated devices, esoteric instruments. We all can know more quickly and, perhaps, more accurately what is wrong, but have little more hope for a cure for cancer, heart disease, diabetes, Alzheimer's, arthritis, and a host of other ailments.

I am angry with the Church also. For thirty years I've been faithful to my calling in preaching, teaching, caring for the flock, ministering to the suffering, supporting with my time, energies, and money the programs and mission of the church-at-large. To be sure, when I entered this calling I recognized there was a price to pay, and I accepted it. In no way could I have imagined the price to be exacted of my family. Bluntly stated, the Church is cheap, and it treats its servants as though they were cheap seconds pulled off the back shelf of humanity. We are discount models with deceiving labels: humble, pious, good, dedicated, and devalued.

The families of many silent pastors suffer in silence. My wife was one of the generous financial supporters of our local congregation. When it came time for a special appeal, she was always ready to respond. When it came to decisions

87

and policy, she had nothing to say. She paid her husband's salary while others decided the course of the church. The power brokers in the local church voice their opinions, manipulate the members, and buy new furniture for their homes, acquire the latest fashions, dine out at the poshest restaurants, and sail away on their cruises. She kept inside the hurt that would not go away.

My hurt doesn't go away either. And the church-at-large has so few resources to which I can turn. Few minister to me in my grief. The ecclesiastical bureaucrats cover their collective sins with a hollow offer: "We'll go out to lunch one of these days." I don't want lunch from the church. I want justice.

I am angry that my wife is taken from me and similarly wrenched from others. And I see so many dumping their spouses. My marriage was ended at the grave; others by a dry courtroom decree. I harbor ill feelings toward a society, and a clergy, that allows marriage partners to split over the smallest incompatibility, where divorce comes in a multitude of flavors, like Baskin Robbins ice cream, where men and women can blame one another and everything except themselves for matrimony's mess. They look for externals over which they have no control and, fingering them, take no responsibility. Their scapegoats play havoc with genuine love and lifetime commitment. Our marriage was probably no model. I suspect none are. It was certainly no fairyland story, no perfect match of endless bliss; it contained no years of uninterrupted happiness. It was, however, the product of our own energies and intentions. We expected nothing else or no one else—good luck, good looks, or the good gods—to make it for us. What we made is now gone, and it all strikes me as sadly unfair.

Months after the initial stages of my grief, little things began to irritate me. What I felt most strongly about were all the small signs that indicated how quickly people around me had abandoned me to my plight. The support quickly vanished. All I heard was the cordial, non-communicative, ritualistic "How are you?" They didn't want to know, or at least, they hoped I would say "I'm fine"—that would relieve them of the burden. I may be wrong, and at times, I hope so, but my suspicions are that my colleagues and companions are neither prepared nor inclined to offer me the opportunity to bare my soul and pain. So I carry it alone, along with my load of resentment.

My anger, I suppose—as irrational as it may sound—is directed more at myself than at anyone else. I am angry with myself precisely because I am so clumsy in expressing and handling this rage. I spread a dank sickness rather than harvest health. Instead of casting out the demons, I pour gasoline on their fires. Walking the line between rage and resignation, between fight and flee, between hate and love, I can only hope my rage is effective, my hate perfect, my love more perfect still.

So I pound my fist, hammer on the walls, slam doors, and shout imprecations. I harbor resentments within and recoil at so many innocent words and gestures. In my curses I can feel the curse of the cross. I wait for the Galilean who comes to me along the shore of the sea, who meets me in the eye of the storm raging within my soul, who turns the tables on an unresponsive society, and casts out the demon named Legion.

9

Time and Times

In the fullness of time God ...
St. Paul

Time like an ever-rolling stream
bears all its sons away
Isaac Watts

The January calendars, those double faces of the New Year, stare blankly across the rooms and spaces they are designed to rule. They are empty, unmarked, inexperienced. The bare months brazenly expose themselves as they flip from season to season, making a vain effort to hold *chronos,* the old crone of time counted. They count nothing, nevertheless; and count for nothing. All their tomorrows, their weekends and Lord's Days, no matter how many emergencies and dates they are bound by duty to keep, are really unknowns, ciphers.

Last year's datebooks and worn-out calendars, on the other hand, hold in them the secrets of our days and months. These are history, and although they may some day turn to dust, they contain the facts that can never be nullified. They are records of *kairos*, the time that fills up with meaning, the time and times that God has supplied with the treasures and trash of our sojourn, the precious cargo and putrid garbage of our journey.

All of it is mixed together, sorted out in little, numbered white boxes; wrapped in a rubber band, tossed into the bottom desk drawer to sleep with 1978, 1983, or whatever. The pictures of Yosemite, red-winged blackbird, Bo Derek, and the Sacred Heart of Jesus over the funeral home directory are merely wrappings. The pencil marks, the circles, "Dinner with Bill," "Dr. Michaels at 2:15," "Taxes due today." These are the events, the occasions, the happenings that fill all the empty boxes and give content to them. They are *kairos* filling *chronos*. These are God and man interacting in spite of the circles of the spheres.

Somehow—and we seem to accept it without question—time must be just right for any particular event. The grunion comes ashore to lay its eggs on California's coasts only on the right tide of the right moon at the right season. The swallows return to Capistrano, the polar bears to Churchill, the salmon to the Skagit River, and the house wren to my back yard. Always at the right time. Baseball cheers and jeers come back to Cincinnati in April without our asking, and Santa Claus to New York on Thanksgiving Day.

All our days are spent as anniversaries of the right times, and we uncork the wine bottles and drink to memories that filled the past. Or we spend those anniversaries trying to forget our age and rage, hoping to lose in the labyrinth of all our monthly records and diaries the dreary story of wine gone sour, of life that has filled June's spaces with thunder clouds instead of sunshine, and September's with forlorn songs.

Grief creates its own myriad anniversaries, and then having pried its way into the space of our lives, claims all the times and seasons. There is neither a right time nor good time for this kind of sorrow even as there is no good or right time for death. It barges onto the stage of our lives at every hour—waking or sleeping—and recites continuously its unmercifully repetitious lines.

Grief, likewise, claims every holiday as its own, and turns the simplest occasion into one. The first day back to work, the first night alone, an evening out for dinner, the Saturday I clean out a closet, that 8:30 P.M. space when I sort out her paperwork and files, the hours I sit with paper and pen, all belong to the grief I can't seem to shake.

I am forced to think of grief in these terms of time and timeliness. When I wonder aloud, "How long?" nodding heads intone, "A long time." I grow weary of the useless toil, the seemingly senseless suffering, the stretched-out anguish, and I want to stretch myself beyond all those little anniversaries my sorrow remembers.

Time and its power catch up to me when others need to express to me their shock and dismay over my wife's death. Their calendars are filled in also, and they in turn, must bring me up-to-date with their feelings and thoughts—something I haven't in my own brooding even considered. When they do, THE EVENT comes back, close and closer, large and larger. That worst night, that horrendous day will not go away, even with time; it hangs tenaciously to me. I can't shake the day, and it persists in filling my future with the past.

Time, at this time, doesn't seem to have the answer to my time. "A time to be born, and a time to die." Only a fool would argue with that. That death will come, finally and inexorably, can't be denied. But must we, on that basis, accept the proposition that every death is timely? Was this the right time for my dear wife to die? I don't know and can't know, and because I can't, the answer is no.

A week before her death I officiated at the burial of a 90-year-old church member. For her grownup sons, older than I, the time of her death still was not right. For them it was painful to say goodbye. If my wife were ninety rather than fifty-two, I might accept her death as timely. Or if she had been suffering, deteriorating, from a long, debilitating disease, I might have seen her dying as appropriate and merciful. But I see her death as a disordering event in the orderly march of days.

I go back to work immediately following the New Year's holiday long yawn. Four morning hours drag torturously before lunchtime breaks up my day. During that dreary morning I keep my mind occupied with busy tasks. Though I attach to them an artificial importance, they are all so trivial: committee assignments, financial reports, bulletin announcements. We convince ourselves that this kind of stuff smells like roses so we don't need to smell sorrow or pluck death. That crazy delusion that time heals all has me staying awake through endless nights and stumbling like a tottering drunk through empty days.

Nothing has been so important in my lifetime as that final event that hastily slammed shut the appointment book of our life together. All the marks on that day's space will mar and smudge all my calendars and pages, the months and days, until God knows when.

And God only knows when.

He obviously knows so much more than I about the time it is and how *kairos* should fill all the little boxes of *chronos*. The skeptic may call it coincidence; Jung coined synchronicity; Rudolf Otto argues for the legitimacy of the numinous; more recently, Scott Peck, in *The Road Less Traveled*, appropriates the word *grace*. Old Simeon had only a glance of the infant Jesus in the temple and knew he was in the right place at the right time, and it was time for his dying, to say good-bye.

Our epiphanies, like Simeon's—those fleeting experiences with God—are all we have with which to decode the scratchings on our calendars. We have only reflected images of God, hints about his presence, we see only his salvation. It is not time to look at him eyeball to eyeball, to see his face, to charge into his holy place. We know neither the time nor the seasons. And I can't know the answer about her death or its timeliness when it looks to me so out of time. I see only the hand of God filling in some of the milli-seconds, the fractions of my lifetime with the events that pull together again the calendar of my days.

Yet an eloquent and mysterious sequence of events tiptoed around the edges of her death and my grief. They had nothing directly to do with her dying, yet, from my perspective, cannot be separated from it. They seem to provide some shadow of God's hand and to some extent, redeem that time.

The day's mail lay on the kitchen table that very afternoon I was struggling with the initial shock of my loss. Among the scattered assortment of bills and junk mail was a strangely-lumpy envelope from a major department store nearby. Searching for some contact with reality, I mechanically went through my mail and opened the envelope. There, to my dismay, was a bundle of long-lost contents from my billfold: pictures, voter's registration, membership cards. The pictures were precious and I felt poor without them—two little girls holding tightly to their young mother, a glamour shot from her beautiful, youthful days, a snapshot of our granddaughter when she was only a day old. And here they were, back in my possession on this singular day. Why did the finder wait two months to return them? What possessed me to mess with the mail on that dark day of sorrow? What does this juxtaposition of events say about time and timeliness?

A day later, another letter, addressed to her, arrived. Once again, merely going through the motions of living, I opened it. It was a photostat copy of a Christmas party announcement sent by one of her classmates at secretarial school. Here was the only telephone number I would find with which I could contact another group of her friends. Without that number none of them would have ever shared in her memory with me.

On the way to the Sunday night memorial service, her best friend and her husband were driving silently through the suburban darkness. He put a tape in the deck to take the edge off their feelings—a recording of a New Orleans jazz band cried the blues through the speakers. The wife pleaded, "Turn that off. It's just not right at a time like this." But he let it play, sweetly singing: "Just a Closer Walk With Thee."

We choose a different kind of music for the service: old hymns of the church, some Bach and Handel. We sat in the front pew awaiting the prelude from the brass quintet as the organist finished an air from *Messiah*. Our friends, sitting in the back, were uncomfortably impressed by what they called a "high class" church service. The quintet, however, didn't begin with Bach's "Little Fugue"; they weren't playing Baroque. They had the effrontery to play jazz—"Just a Closer Walk With Thee." God, in his own time, touched these friends with a gift of synchronicity, and faith.

The following December nights were terribly long, awfully blank. My daughter and I, now alone, would sit together in our remorse and thoughts. We reflected silently, sometimes aloud, sharing our pain, our dashed hopes, our sorrow for her. I pulled from the ceiling-high bookcase a volume I had given my wife as a Christmas gift a few years before. It was a collection of poems by Edna St. Vincent Millay, somber

97

and serious with the thoughts of death, dark and deep as her most private thoughts. I let the book fall open to page 111, breaking into the middle of one of her longer poems, and I read lines that I might have written myself that night:

> *I long for Silence as they long for breath*
> *Whose helpless nostrils drink the bitter sea;*
> *What thing can be*
> *So stout, what so redoubtable, in Death*
> *What fury, what considerable rage, if only she,*
> *Upon whose icy breast,*
> *Unquestioned, uncaressed,*
> *One time I lay,*
> *And whom always I lack,*
> *Even to this day,*
> *Being by no means from that frigid bosom weaned away,*
> *If only she therewith be given me back.*
> Collected Poems, Edna St. Vincent Millay, Norman Millay, *ed., New York:*
> *Harper & Row*

The author was thinking about silence; I about death. The words fit both occasions.

So did the words I found underscored in her old Bible. I had been rummaging through some dresser drawers—one of the inescapable tasks death brings upon us—when I stumbled upon the brittle red cover and drying Indian paper. I had given it to her on Easter in 1954. Once again I looked

at the first page that fell open, to the few lines underlined
with red pencil:

But I would not have you to be ignorant,
brethren, concerning them which are asleep,
that ye sorrow not, even as others which have no hope.
For if we believe that Jesus died and rose again,
even so them which also sleep in Jesus
will God bring with him.
1 Thessalonians 4:13-14, KJV

So in my darkest hours there were some moments, some
flashes of light. I can only believe that God somehow was
leading me to see these times as a starting place for hope.

The days drag into weeks, and the weeks stretch into
months. I grow weary from the passing of time, waiting for
the day when I shall at last enjoy sucking in a breath of fresh
air, when I can spontaneously laugh, when I can welcome
these silent evenings as my private, individual life. For the
present, I go on living out of a sense of duty. I brush my
teeth, watch my diet, try to exercise, change the bed, do the
laundry and tend to a whole list of trivial tasks. They have no
real meaning for me, but I obey the impulse to get the jobs
done, as absurd as they seem. I am cried out; I feel numb,
almost indifferent; I am thinking through, rather than feeling
this grief. The exhausting, wrenching, acuteness of sorrow
could last only so long. Perhaps that is time's major contribu-

tion. I don't see any happy ending yet, nor do I feel my grief being yet resolved. No teleological answer for her death comes forward; time just creeps toward its own end.

Living a life that I haven't chosen, merely going through the motions, nonetheless I have learned to begin to live each of my days in the present. Even though I mechanically push the shopping cart through the market's cluttered aisles, pay the bills that keep knocking at the door, attend to every desultory task, I am at least living today. Each action is detached from yesterday's hurt; each task is separate from the vain wishes I hold for a bright tomorrow.

This present moment moves farther and farther away from that undying past, however, and closer to that future, whatever it may bring. Every breath I take, every minute I am awake, every hour I work, widens the margin between the old reality and a new one. In that way, time does its gentle, gracious work.

10

Depression

All flesh is grass,
and all its beauty is like
the flowers of the field
Isaiah

Her tears fell with the dews at even;
Her tears fell ere the dews were dried.
Tennyson

The low sun casts exaggerated shadows across the frozen
landscape as Candlemas marks the midpoint of this cruel
season. The planetary clockwork, like some meteorological
turnaround, strikes a quiet gong, signaling to us a real spring
and summer. But the groundhog, shadow or not, brings me
no solace. The winter solstice lies far behind, the vernal
equinox calls to me with her green velvet voice, but I cannot
hear. Something inside me raises its own racket and gnaws
away; a persistent ache robs me of inspiration, saps me of

energy. Other voices from the past deafen me to spring's song.

Winter is made for remembering. Just as spring is for planting and summer for blooming, or autumn for tasting the fruit of our labors, winter is simply for looking back. This winter recalls for me our early years together, the "freeze-outs" we experienced in the more northern latitudes of Michigan and the foothills of New York's Adirondack Mountains. It paints our past in the snow that lies blue and steel gray on the still earth, going nowhere, every new flake adding to the fall from the day before. I see in the flashbacks my young wife bundled up against the bitter cold, standing in hip-deep snow, hanging diapers on the clothesline, her fingers frozen. I see her at her sewing machine (for which we paid $2.00 a week), zipping together tiny coats and warm togs for our children. I see her kneading dough and baking homemade bread and cinnamon rolls; I smell an apple pie in the oven; I hear her practicing hymns on the old piano in the parlor. I watch her come home weary after a day at work in the department store earning a few more dollars to supplement a meager income, and to assure us a few day trips in the summer and autumn. There were no vacation jaunts in those days.

We were young then, and we saw life somewhere out in front of us. When we would ever catch up with it was uncertain. She saw big and bright stars in my future—far bigger and brighter than I would expect—and some day soon those stars would be within reach…. Then, in one unsuspected moment, a single star spun off into some far-off galactic night and twinkled its last point of light. The darkness settled upon me like the ashes of a spent comet.

For us together, all is now past, nothing lies ahead; only the dim and distant hope of a new star rising in God's tomorrow, on this gray morning too far for me to see. I hope and pray that somehow God in his infinite wisdom and mercy will cause the sun to shine on me and restore to me joy and gladness, to pull me out of this night of suffering, to haul my soul out of that distant past and all those wet-eyed memories. I hope that it will be soon. But not too soon. Why not so soon? Because I need to hold on to something I know. The most genuine feeling I own is my aching longing, my painful yearning, my impish Eros. I am homesick. I want to go back to that cozy, warm embrace of all that I once knew.

How can I expect others to enter with me into this homesickness? Their lives, happy or miserable, are pretty well settled and they are "at home." Each morning brings for them familiar smiles—or arguments; and night, their reveries of domestic warmth—or warfare. Either way, their lives are filled with well-known contents. Mine is now an empty room. The furniture is cleaned out; pictures are removed from the walls leaving their outlines on the faded paint; lamps, books, knick-knacks, even the dust, is gone. Am I empty? Or do I simply struggle to find my way in an empty, colorless space without landmarks or reference points? Death empties us of all our treasures, of everything that fits like the old shoe, of all the landmarks that tell us where we are. Grief is the struggle to find the way when we are far from home.

As the long night drags on, my grief takes on new drab colors and deranged shapes. I am homesick most of all, but mixed in with that element of grief, and all hardly distinguishable from the other in one stretched-out, homogenized journey, are compulsion, apathy, and spiritual dullness.

Will God, to whom I pray in rationed-out trickles, show me the way? Is he the one who will fill up the holes bored into the structure of my journey on earth? Who is this God who leaves me in such a spiritual vacuum? Perhaps the voice of Job's wife is the most honest voice in all the Bible: "Curse God, and die."

I find I can't do that, but neither does my bereavement drive me to my knees in devotion, or turn me to the pages of Scripture, or walk hand-in-hand with a benevolent Father. My experience corresponds with so many who feel the same deprivation of spiritual resources. We find it increasingly difficult to hear the Word of God, and we fall dumb at the hour of prayer. It is as though God were on some space journey and has suddenly veered off in the direction of the most distant stars.

Death defies all our deepest spiritual imagery. The promise of a future heavenly home takes a back seat to the harsh, present homesickness. I can't talk or think about heaven until I've dealt firmly and courageously with the finality of her physical death. She's dead and buried, and I can hardly get myself to write that line, to say those words. She is gone and nothing can bring her back to me, and spiritual language gives me no answers. It only leaves me longing.

Perhaps that is one of death's gifts. Now I realize God is not the image I have fashioned; He doesn't correspond to the shape of my sculpture. He is not a catalog of answers for my myriad questions, or Band-Aids for my multiple hurts and sores. The presence of death forces us into a different spirituality—one that struggles with a God we can't really know, whose holiness is his distinctive "beyondness," whose likeness fits none of our molds and meets none of our preconceived demands. He is the one who thunders from the mountaintops or whispers in the cleft of the rock, who rides the storm and tames the stampeding tempest, who dresses himself in the glory of the heavens that stretch from sky to sky. Separating himself from the picture gallery of Canaan's iconography, he never shows his face.

Religion may provide the answers science cannot know, and it solves the problems that lie beyond technology's ken, but we can't tie God down to that kind of religion. Too often our notions of God turn Him into one who makes up for our lack of understanding and knowledge. When God is simply what we on our own can't know, then such is an idol indeed, not the God of Abraham, Isaac, and Jacob, and the Father of our Lord Jesus Christ, not the creator of heaven and earth, the Alpha and the Omega. Not the God who answers Job from the whirlwind or Isaiah from the flaming altar.

I believe death and grief are harder on a believer because they present him with new difficulties. God, who seems to have forsaken the Christian, now becomes Himself a problem for which there is no solution. So we weep at the great affirmations of faith; we choke on the hymns of the church; we lose our grip in our flights of prayer. The Word doesn't ring clear as it always had, our prayers are worn thin, the creeds become hollow dogma. And we feel spiritless, and spiritually alone. Grief is a sojourn in a secular city where God lies entombed, from whose burial mounds we must rise and take a new journey of genuine faith, affirm death first, then move on from there to life.

This very frustration with our personal faith and our images of God also is the renewal of faith and hope. Neither a Cartesian description of heaven nor an empirical proof for life beyond death constitutes our hope. We cannot fill our future with the material of our dreams, or with what we think we know. It is precisely because the future is so barrenly empty, that we are so uncertain about it, that we can face it with hope. Hope reaches out to the God of promise who will fill his own tomorrows. And that future, as dim as it seems, is ours.

It is this God, whose essence is promise, who becomes immanent in my prayerless days and my spiritless nights. Absent and present in the cross, he is both far and near as I struggle with faith and unbelief. "Lord, I believe; help my unbelief."

I am homesick, I am spiritually empty, and I am weary. Months of grief sap one's energy, exhaust all physical and mental powers, drain one of every ounce of reserve. As the months go by, I find myself accommodating to the realities that surround me. I mechanically tend to the callings of the home, the demands put upon my gray days, the exigencies that translate into more than mere existence. I plod along through the mud; it sticks to my shoes; each step becomes heavier and heavier. Mourning is a long, slow, ponderous walk.

The waves of grief of which I had written earlier continue to rise and fall, but the fury is not so noticeable, the surf no longer so wild, the troughs not so deep. The ocean of sorrow begins to flatten out, I become accustomed to the gentle, predictable rolling of the sea. The ripples on the surface spread in every direction, they seemingly go on forever in a monotonous rhythm. Occasionally, I am lifted to something close to elation, somewhere in the vicinity of happiness, almost to that height where I can hear laughter and song. And similarly, I am lowered, ever so little, to where the tears well up, where the old wounds open, and recent pains register familiar throbs. But the gale is gone, the energy is spent, the fire is cooled, the ennui covers me, suffocates me.

For the months following my wife's death, I made especially hard work of meeting the challenges of my new task. I resumed my work as a pastor and preacher. I planned meals and cooked for myself. I managed to keep the house looking somewhat respectable, stocked the larder, saw to old and new details, even made room for some recreation, visitors, friends. This new and foreboding life without her stared me in the eye and dared me to master it. So I went at it as best I could. At first I felt a tinge of triumph. Then the whole arrangement of challenge, duty, sorrow, life, death began to fit. The hurts and the despair became a garment I found myself wearing too well. Indeed, facing head-on these daily foes became a dragging bore. Anguish gave way to ennui, loneliness to lassitude, bereavement to boredom. It is in this long drawn-out stage that creativity evades me. I find myself drifting, making few decisions, and even those few with difficulty, wallowing in a shallow kind of depression, just "hanging in there."

The winter snows have been long melted, leaving their traces of gray scum on fresh, green grass reaching for the brighter rays of sunlight. The time for sowing has come and gone as though I've never taken notice. The oppressive heat now bears down on us, our speed slows, our minds grow numb to the drone of fans and air conditioners. Picnics and cook-outs cram our calendars. I creep at a snail's pace through the humid days and long for cool, sleeping nights. By the time I arrive to pluck summer's blooms, the flowers have faded and they are gone. And I wonder: when shall I enjoy the harvest?

11

Resolution

Fear not, I am the first and the last,
and the living one;
I died, and behold, I am alive for evermore.
The Apocalypse

Come now, solemnest feast on the road
to eternal freedom,
Death, and destroy those fetters that bow,
those walls that imprison this
"our transient life."
Dietrich Bonhoeffer

I can't bring her back. I cannot undo what is done, or change the inexorable march of time. Yet there remains within my soul the compelling need to do something to justify, to make right, even to avenge her death. This is the fourth shape my grief takes. Compulsion, that insatiable driving force within, accompanies homesickness, spiritual apathy, and, ambiguously as it may seem, ennui and indifference. In my case this compelling quest began at the outset, sometimes as rage, sometimes as remorse, always real. The torpor that came along later took the edge of this passion, but the compelling need continues to make itself felt.

One of the reasons for this unfulfilled drive, I believe, is our culture's lack of ritual with which to deal effectively with death and dying. We have become experts in denial, believing to our very last gasp in miracle drugs and supernatural surgery, in our essential immortality, in the fables that convince us it won't happen here. Death is disguised by dignified designers who speak in hushed tones and peddle all the comforts of the grave. We dignify death by trying our earthly best to make something innocuous of it; we rob the dying of dignity by insisting they keep living even when life is no longer reasonable. Perhaps, with more studies, more literature on death and dying, there are promises of all this changing. We have, however, a long way to go. We need to uncork the bottles that are charged with all the feelings, the misgivings, the fears that attend grief. We need to adopt a new set of rules that says it is acceptable to die, and appropriate to suffer over death, that allows the spilling out of all the explosive, fermenting pressures.

I also feel the compulsion arise when my own needs go unmet. No one can take her place. Words, especially, fall far short of ameliorating the hurt. Most people who brush by the fringe of my life have only words. What I need is something at a more primal level. I need touch, contact, tears, feelings from others.

Could I ever discover an answer for her death? For months I felt driven to uncover every clue, decipher every little past gesture, put together the scrambled bits and pieces of the jigsaw puzzle that made up the days preceding her self-destruction. I would be that detective who would sift through every piece of evidence, look at each nuance from its odd angle, ask the same questions over and over: When? What? Where? I would add it all up and come up with the *Why*. However, all I had in the end was information, not an answer.

Through this struggle I learned that information would be of little help. Information about what Christians believe might comfort me for a moment; information about her mental anguish might take the edge off her early death; information about my still living in a world full of possibilities might even lift my spirits. But it is still information, more of the same, piled on what has become a glut in our society. I found myself dealing with death and sorrow as though it could be programmed for the computer. The data would be devoured, churned, digested, and eventually the machines would spit out the answer. It doesn't work.

Please don't give me words; give me a hug. Don't tell me that I'm holding up so well; break down with me and admit our shared wretchedness. Don't feign some bright mountain-top; walk with me through the dark valley where neither of us can utter a word.

What I need is a non-rational response. I do not mean irrational. Irrational responses are inappropriate operations of our rational, abstract, left-brained-ness. The non-rational

She Never Said Good-bye

comes from another hemisphere, another place in our marvelous makeup, a place we too infrequently visit. When we do, however, we find some resolution to our puzzles.

One winter day my daughter, who has few words about her grief or my own, provided one of those eloquent statements I needed. It was a short time after Christmas when she brought home a record album about which neither of us knew much. We placed the disc on the record player and silently listened to the outpouring of Gustav Mahler's Second Symphony—the Resurrection Symphony. To me the music of Mahler is powerful and moving and requires an attentive ear. I could feel myself sink and rise; I could see the dark passages and the light; I could sense death and resurrection in notes and sounds. Concluding with intensifying choral music—here sung in German and therefore out of my reach—the symphony was not a verbal or logical message to me. Instead, I had caught a deep feeling from the music, the non-rational "word"; I was transported somehow to the creation and the new creation. The music lifted the curtain from around my soul. "That is it," I said, and said no more. Words would only garble up the truth I so desperately sought. Here, in the pit of bereavement, I could only feel the truth. And I felt a compelling need to do something that would keep that moment of truth alive.

Did there yet remain something I could do, however? Something more than listening to good music, or watching promising sunsets? Was there more than just an accepting attitude, as crucial as that is? As time wore on, the prospects

112

of finding that secret act whereby I could undo what was done, seemed more and more remote. My rage has subsided considerably, and vengeance was never my goal. Yet, for want of a better word, I continued to feel the need to avenge her tragic death. I sought some mythic paradigm that would yield a universal answer to all the questions that dangle before my mind. The Greeks had their Oedipus and Prometheus. James Joyce could cast a reflection of his own face from the likenesses of Icarus and Dedalus. In our modern age we are called upon to avenge the death of the gods by slaying mother, with all her comforts and securities, and take responsibility for the consequences in the uncertain life ahead—without God and without mother. Like Orestes, it is important for me to latch onto some responsible act so that I too can say unequivocally: "I did it. I can blame no one else for the life I live, the pain I bear, the suffering I endure."

I cannot take responsibility for history. I can only take charge of myself, my feelings, my words and actions. I can assume the blame for my own stupidity or laziness and even take credit for my achievements. Orestes doesn't go far enough; I must leave to God the outcome of history.

That outcome of human history, that beginning and end, also comes to us in mythical language—the language of drama and apocalypse. Significant to our struggles with death is the biblical story of that primordial, first death, the murder of Abel (Genesis 4:1-16). All wrapped up into one small package is the human situation: disapproval, shame, jealous rage, intrigue, fratricide, denial, anxiety, alienation.

Cain was caught in his crime and feared for his life. He saw himself as a fugitive running and hiding from everyone who would avenge his brother's death. Who they were who would kill Cain is merely silly speculation and hardly germane to the story. Cain's death would end human history. Without that threat, the story is just one more tragic tale. God, therefore, put a mark on Cain's head to preserve and keep him in the land of Nod, east of Eden. In Eden we fall from grace; but East of Eden we go on living and survive, by grace.

The last book of the Bible, filled with portents and threatening storms, tells the story of how God, not man, will bring to completion human history. It is God who brings barbarous Babylon to her knees. The defeat of the great harlot is the hope of all the saints, of Israel, of every Abel and Cain. God will avenge the death of all whose death brings pain and grief. He will call to task the bitter turns of our own history, and because of this divine intervention, we may take responsibility for our own lives within the province of his grace, under the aegis of the mark of Cain.

I am letting go. I am giving her into the gracious hands of an infinitely loving God who raised from the dead our Lord Jesus. I leave Christ to avenge her death and the deaths of every martyr and saint. I leave behind me the compelling need to know all the whys and wherefores. I leave death where it belongs, where someday the shadow of the cross will illuminate the dark nimbus that cloaks the land of Cain.

My responsibility is not to justify death—hers or anyone's. Mine is to resolve this prolonged episode of grief, to discover whether, by some slim chance, there may still be a happy ending to the story. As I live in this present moment, so often empty and joyless, I inadvertently move farther and farther from that past. As I wait out my days, I am drawn closer only when it succeeds in blocking the continuity of the past with the future. History cannot be obliterated, scenes still flash before my eyes, memories linger. And I also dream and aspire to brighter mornings, to wake up to birds singing, to the redolence of flower gardens, to a life unburdened by such heavy sorrow and aloneness. My present experiences must drive a wedge between that too-familiar past and that unimaginable future.

It takes courage to take charge in one's grief, but the alternative is to be overcome by it. As I reflect on my own, I have come to appreciate that its resolution has its own price tag and I must be willing to pay that price or I shall be forever paying. Part of that price is the willingness to let go in order to start over again.

This need for indomitable courage became apparent to me after about seven months of mourning. Surely there is no special time schedule for any particular grief experience. Every one is different, each circumstance varies, every episode of loss has its own idiosyncrasies. I simply remember that a span of time had to elapse before I woke up to a new reality: I am no longer a married man. (The day I write these lines an invitation to a conference for single clergy arrived in the mail.) I can no longer derive my sense of being from my wife. She is no longer a part of me, painful as it is to face that agonizing fact. I must discover *me,* and allow myself to grow from whatever bud or cocoon this experience is.

The price is paid when we take new directions and reorient this life that for now is spinning in ever-tightening circles. A greater courage arises when we launch out in some direction without the compass. We pay that price when we get in motion, when we budge off dead center. It is a frightening step to begin re-ordering this life. We are assured it is in process, however, as we feel grief fade into mourning, when foolish guilt turns into acceptable remorse, when our shock gives way to a more stable reality. We move even further along the way when courage usurps the place of self-pity and pathos, when our direction points outward rather than inward, when love is a genuine focus in life again.

If there is anything I can do to avenge her horrible death, my unthinkable loss, it is to move in this new direction. The single most important object of my love, sullied and shallow as that love may be, is gone. She has been torn from my presence. Sickening and heart-wrenching as it is to be denied her love, it is as impoverishing to lose the one to whom I direct mine. Because there is no object, there seems to be no love. For this reason I want to hold on to her, I want to "stay married." I must release her to where love is made perfect, however, and reach out to where it is still possible for me.

So I, in part, avenge her death and resolve my grief by following our Lord's commandment, "Love one another." Death calls us to act out this gift, to love our neighbor, our families, the unlovely and unlovable, Cain the killer, whoever our brother may be.

The author of that new mandate, the regnant prince of the Apocalypse, can leave us with that commandment for he is the one who died and lives forevermore. He conquers death and the grave.

The New Testament uses two words for death: *necrosis* and *thanatos*. The former, taken over by medical science, refers to the degeneration of cells and tissues, the dying away of organs of the body and eventually the entire organism. In its broadest sense, *necrosis* is the rule of nature: from dust we have come and to dust we shall return. The dead are called *nekron*.

Christ joined the *nekron* in the awful agony of the cross, the cessation of all cellular processes, the closing down of each organ's operation—breathing, circulation, brain activity—were all a part of his dying. He was raised from *nekron*, according to the Scriptures, and thereby conquered death. *Thanatos* could not hold him.

I walk side-by-side with lengthening days and the ineluctable march of time. The lightheartedness of springtime has slipped through my fingers like drops of April rain. The dog days of summer press heavily upon me, and with them new memorials to her passing: her birthday stares incongruously into my face. What meaning can birth have once death steps in?

I sort through her clothing and personal effects, dispose of some, hold on to others as a link to her active, creative, living past. Then, in the midst of August's fading glow, a gray, drizzly morning greets our wedding anniversary. I can't share the day with a soul; I mention it to no one. Alone I carry red roses to her resting place and let *necrosis* clutch at my throat and burn my eyes. Here I come to grips once again with the finality of her dying; once again I leave myself to the purging effects of catharsis; once again I am face to face with the dead.

There are no faces; not a voice is heard. The clouds shield me from late summer's searing heat; a few drops of rain ruffle the parched grass and mingle with my tears. I stand in the land of the dead, *nekron*, where all return to the same dust. There are no outstanding dead here; all have the same sized graves, all the same flat markers. They come from the corners of the earth, carried by the floodtide of immigrants seeking a better life—and achieving a common death. Their names are spelled out: Van Horn, Gianetti, Avignon, Ahern, Anagnostakos, Schwaeble, Kozlay, Johannsen, Zivkovich, Shannon, Davis, Kramer, Dykstra. Here are the *nekron*. Here *necrosis* becomes a stage in the natural order of things. It is all part of a grand cycle which to deny is to court an illusion.

118

Nevertheless, here at the edge of her grave the supremely natural inches over into the supernatural. All the cemeteries, memorial parks, old graveyards and ancient burial mounds wrap us together in a single shroud of wonder.

Here death becomes *thanatos*, diametrically opposed to life. It is the ancient enemy that goes far beyond wearing down cells and tissue. It flies in the face of everything God designs. Her death screams at me, and I scream in reply. It is no friend that has visited me out of some sweet, sentimental past. It is a hardened foe against which I continue to battle. I cannot let *thanatos* lie comfortably under the quiet sods of *nekrosis*. Death must not and will not reign!

The grave, silent and cold, not the fiery, red-hot images of Armageddon, carries me into the last age, the final day, the single tomorrow of the conquering Christ. The victorious death and resurrection of the Son of Man alone frees me to live in the face of death, to accept her dying—and my own— as a purely natural consequence of living. It calls me to till my garden of memories and dreams. Where once the rising eastern sun cast its long, dreadful shadows across the face of Paradise, it now signals a bright, undying hope.